IncentShare®

Motivate, Recruit, and Get Results
with Incentives

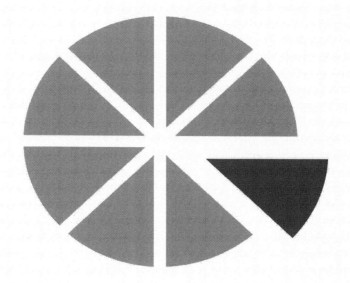

Succeed by Sharing

Keith, Thanks for Sharing! Rob

Rob Marchalonis

Info@IncentShare.com

IncentShare, c/o VDP123 LLC Publishing,
1653 Lititz Pike, #222, Lancaster, PA 17601
www.IncentShare.com

Ordering Information:
Special discounts are available for quantity purchases by businesses and organizations.
For details, contact the publisher as shown above.

ISBN: 099871030X
ISBN 13: 9780998710303

Important Disclaimer

This book contains information and materials that are designed to help readers assess the merits of business ideas and are for educational purposes only. Extra effort has been made to identify and verify that the information in this publication is accurate and up to date; however, the author and publisher assume no responsibility for any inaccuracy, omission, error, or otherwise. This book and its content are not intended to guarantee or represent that you will achieve the desired results, and the author and publisher make no such guarantee. Neither the author nor publisher shall be liable for any damages resulting from any ideas, suggestions, recommendations, or other information included, referenced, or implied in this publication. Every business, organization, and employment arrangement comes with risks.

Employment and compensation practices are governed by various laws and government regulations. No information or recommendations in this book or by the author, publisher, or their representatives are intended to supersede applicable laws or regulations. Neither the author, publisher, or any of their representatives are legal or accounting advisors. It is strongly advised that you consult with both legal and accounting professionals before implementing or making changes to any compensation plan or acting on any information provided in this publication.

The names and addresses of websites, Internet locations, and other resources were included before publication as a reference. They are not intended in any way to imply or be an endorsement, and there is no way to ensure their accuracy or availability after publication. The author and publisher have no control over and assume no responsibility for websites or other third-party resources.

Some parts of this book reflect the author's best-present recollection of past experiences. The names and descriptions of some people, organizations, and events in this book have been changed to protect privacy.

Thank You.
This book is dedicated to my family,
mentors, coworkers, clients, and friends who, by
sharing
their inspiration, wisdom, resources, leadership, and love,
have blessed and provided incentive to me in ways
more amazing than they can ever know.

"

Share your profits with all your associates, and treat them as partners. In turn, they will treat you as a partner, and together you will all perform beyond your wildest expectations.

"

Sam Walton - founder of Walmart

Contents

"

The miracle is this: The more we share the more we have.

"

Leonard Nimoy - actor, director, and Spock

Welcome

This book was written to help you consider, design, and implement custom employee-compensation plans based on incentives and sharing. Incentives will motivate your team and boost your results. Yes, there are lots of ways to motivate a workforce, but none are as powerful as sharing your success with the team that will get you there.

If you can find a way to share a portion of your success—a plan where your team will benefit because of the gains or improvements they help create—you can unleash the amazing potential in your employees. When results and success are shared, people rise to new levels and perform their best.

Incentives will help you tap into the enormous abilities and capacity of your employees, especially when they work as a team. When success is shared you will find that effort, teamwork, and productivity can rise significantly, resulting in better outcomes, results, and prosperity for all stakeholders.

An age-old concept reemerging. Sharing the fruit *of* the labor *with* the labor is a powerful concept with references back to Biblical times. The apostle Paul guided Timothy and his followers about money and its temptations by offering these instructions: "Tell them to use their money to do good. They should be rich in good works and generous to those in need, always being ready to *share* with others" (1 Timothy 6:18 NLT). I believe that Paul's instructions were much more than altruistic; they were also a model for healthy workplaces and sustainable businesses. Today, wise leaders are continuing to do good and succeed by sharing.

There is hardly a company celebrated in the news or whose products you have come to enjoy and admire that doesn't share in some creative way with employees. Many do this as a core strategy to promote innovation and performance.

Google, Facebook, Twitter, Tesla, Blue Apron, and other high and low-tech start-ups were launched by young talent with a significant amount of "skin in the game." It's impossible to know exactly how much the founders and early employees were driven by challenge, opportunity, purpose, or money. Certainly, the hardworking pioneers in these and other headline-making companies were significantly motivated by how much they would eventually benefit in proportion to the success of their businesses.

Consider Starbucks. The coffee company, with over 23,000 stores and 238,000 employees, has created one of the most recognized, respected, and customer-loyal brands in the world. A key to accomplishing this has been providing each customer with a unique Starbucks experience in welcoming and comfortable environments delivered through superior customer service. Accomplishing this isn't easy. One of the ways Starbucks has succeeded is by strategically sharing with their employees, who they call partners, through "Bean Stock." Employee-partners, from baristas to executives in the boardroom, all participate. Eligible partners are granted restricted stock units annually, which change to shares of Starbucks stock after a period of time. Through this sharing process, employees increasingly *own* more and more of the business and share proportionally in its growth and success.[1,2]

At Chobani, the upstate New York manufacturer of packaged yogurt, more than 2,000 employees were recently given a stake in the company by founder Hamdi Ulukaya. The goal, he stated, was to pass along the wealth that employees have helped to build in the decade since the business was started *and* to inspire them to continue to work and build the company and their future at the same time. Built on the premise of "better food for more people," Chobani has become the #1 yogurt brand in America according to its website. Mr. Ulukaya, a Turkish immigrant, reportedly shared up to 10 percent of the privately held company, distributed among full-time employees based on their length of time in the business, to be granted when the company goes public or is sold. Since the company started in 2005, in part with the purchase of a defunct Kraft yogurt plant and an $800,000 loan, the business is now reportedly worth several billion dollars. At this valuation, Chobani employees could enjoy six-figure payouts.[3]

Apple, the computer company, created a program in 2015 to award restricted stock (shares that typically vest over a specific period of time) to hourly paid workers. Benefits like this are often limited to executives, managers, and engineers to engage and more closely connect them to the company and its performance. Apple's annual report claimed that roughly half of its employees work in retail stores, many of whom are paid hourly. While it's common for tech company startups to attract and retain talent with stock awards, this practice is not usually shared among hourly paid employees.[4]

Uber and Lyft are among the newest and most successful businesses built on a sharing model. These businesses generate revenue by connecting riders and drivers, typically via phone app or computer, which is then shared between the driver and the company. Drivers, who work as independent subcontractors, report that their share of each fare is around 75–80%, minus some transaction fees and expenses. Surge pricing during busy periods—up to and beyond three times the normal rates—and various perks and bonuses help to offset the expense and risk that come with the job. To ensure quality and protect the interests of each party, both riders and drivers are encouraged to rate the experience and each other. Drivers with ratings that fall below a relatively high standard are removed from the driver pool. Many successful drivers claim that they most enjoy the freedom to work when and where they prefer and the opportunity to strategically plan, learn, and optimize how to deliver win-win-win outcomes for the riders, the company, and themselves.

Sharing as a core business strategy is not new or reserved only for the newest or biggest. I'd venture to guess that your favorite hometown restaurant hums with energy from a motivated service staff. These waiters, waitresses, bartenders, and others are eager to serve you, knowing that the tip you share with them will be directly linked to the food, care, and service they deliver. The best of them are also mindful that you have a choice of where you dine, and the fact that your return to their restaurant time after time can provide continued and potentially bigger rewards.

From centuries-old wisdom in the Bible to present-day practices at behemoths like Berkshire Hathaway and fast-growing companies like Blue Apron, sharing is a strategy that successful leaders and organizations have used to grow and prosper. Learn more in the pages ahead about how business owners, organization leaders, customers, clients, employees, and *you* can benefit by IncentSharing.

"

If you pick the right people and give them the opportunity to spread their wings and put compensation as a carrier behind it you almost don't have to manage them.

"

Jack Welch - 20 yr. CEO of General Electric

Boost Your Results

If you are reading this, it likely means you are considering or have attempted some type of incentive or variable compensation plan for your employees. Congratulations! We believe you will discover that no other approach is as simple or as effective to boost the focus, morale, teamwork, and success of your workforce.

Are you a leader? If so, what is your plan for success? Business, nonprofit, and other organization leaders *must* deliver results. Among your top challenges are determining *what* results to achieve, a *way* to achieve them, *who* is best suited to do the work, and *how* to engage and encourage peak performance. If you have established a vision and some goals, created a plan or strategy, and assembled a team, you are off to a good start. But there's another step, a critical gap that you must bridge:

How You Seed and Develop Motivation in the Hearts and Minds of Your Team Will Likely Be the Biggest Factor that Determines Your Success or Failure.

Variable compensation, based on performance, is a proven way to improve the results of your organization. When the compensation of teams and individuals can go up or down based on results, outcomes often change significantly for the better. Variable compensation plans are a powerful motivator, but they must be planned and implemented carefully. Typically they look something like:

(Base Pay) +

(Incentive Pay based on Result A) +

(Incentive Pay based on Result B) =

A Variable Compensation Plan

The structure of variable compensation plans can be customized in a number of ways. Each of the components above, (Base Pay) + (Incentive Pay), can have just one or multiple elements that can be linked to various results and factors. I personally have created hundreds of different incentive approaches and sharing formulas designed to meet the specific needs, objectives, and goals of various work groups and organizations. Well-structured plans take into consideration the size of your opportunities, the makeup of your workforce, your current approach to motivation and engagement, the ways you measure performance, and various options to share a portion of your success with all or part of your team. Effectiveness, simplicity, and flexibility are the fundamental goals for any variable compensation plan.

Integrity Is Essential.

It should go without saying, however I want to be very clear that any variable compensation, incentive, or sharing plan must reward and ensure behavior of the highest integrity among all participants.

It's simply wrong—and bad business—to structure any compensation plan that encourages, rewards, or even allows unethical, immoral, or questionable employee behaviors. Preventing these negative outcomes may be the most important among the many reasons that compensation plans should be carefully designed, monitored, and enforced.

The Wells Fargo fiasco. You likely have heard or read about the mess that surfaced at Wells Fargo bank in 2016 as a result of seemingly misguided, poorly managed, and ethically wrong customer practices.

Wells Fargo, a very large and generally well-respected financial institution, suffered a loss well beyond embarrassment in mid-2016 when it was discovered that some of the bank's employees had cut corners and opened deposit and credit card accounts for customers without their knowledge or approval. According to financial reporting from *Forbes*,[5] the practices supposedly occurred from 2011 or earlier and continued until mid-2016 as a result of weak leadership practices or poorly designed incentives. Apparently, more than one and a half million unauthorized deposit accounts were created along with 500,000 unauthorized credit card applications. *What?*

How could this happen at one of the oldest and formerly most respected banking institutions? A poorly designed incentive system may have been to blame. Seemingly, bank branch workers were given aggressive sales goals, quotas, and rewards (or punishment) that prompted behaviors that were unanticipated, conveniently overlooked, or maliciously managed.

The *Forbes* report indicated that the deceptively created accounts generated $2,600,000 in fees for Wells. A large number, but insignificant in comparison to the personal, financial, and reputation costs the bank has only begun to pay. For starters, in an attempt to put the issue behind them, Wells Fargo executives announced the bank would pay $185,000,000 in fines to city and federal regulators in preemptive response to likely lawsuits. Prior to this decision, about 5,300 bank workers had lost their jobs for creating the phony accounts. Treasury officials and banking regulators called Wells CEO John Stumpf on the government carpet in September of 2016 and blasted him for shoddy practices under his watch. The smooth-talking and formerly respected bank chief ultimately could neither dodge nor escape the public's or his board of directors' wrath, and announced his retirement less than sixty days later, supposedly losing $41,000,000 in clawbacks of unvested stock awards. How long will it take for this iconic banking institution to restore an immeasurable amount of lost client trust—an investment that had compounded over years of company history that burst like a bubble as a result of poorly planned incentives and questionable leadership? Ouch, ouch, and ouch.

What can we learn from Wells Fargo? Never compromise your personal integrity or the integrity of your company or employer by creating, allowing, or overlooking incentive practices that are anything but ethical and honorable. Whatever real or perceived business challenges you face, there's no benefit nor reason to risk being the subject of multiple customer complaints let alone national headlines like Wells Fargo bank did.

IncentShare Was Written to Help You Assess, Plan, Design, Implement, and Evolve Custom Compensation Plans.

Language Matters

Open your mind to a keyword and powerful concept. As you read through this book and learn more about variable compensation and incentive plans, I encourage you to keep an open mind. Put aside for a moment your perceptions or previous experience with compensation plans and consider a keyword and powerful concept.

"Sharing" Is the Keyword.

"Success Sharing" Is the Key Concept.

To apply the concept of success sharing within an organization, two things must happen. First, success must be defined and quantified. Second, an appropriate method of success sharing must be created that proportionally benefits both the organization and the participants. It's a simple win-win idea:

"The more successful we are, the more we can share, and the more we share, the more successful we will become."

The language you use is important, because it's often the most visible and frequent expression of your intent. We advocate "sharing" language rather than "incentives" to best express the mutual benefit to both the organization *and* employees, the sharing participants. Keep in mind that for some, the word "incentive" carries connotations of manipulation or short-term enticement. Many have been wounded by incentive approaches that were attractive up-front but which ultimately resulted in back-end or long-term disappointment because of selfish motives, poor planning, inadequate structure, or weak execution. Be mindful of your intent as well as the language you use to communicate why and how you want to share your organization's success:

Incentives, Rewards, Variable Compensation = GOOD

Sharing, Success Sharing, Results Sharing = BETTER

IncentSharing = BEST

Moving forward, I will use the term IncentShare as a noun to describe this book and my resource website, IncentShare.com. I may occasionally use IncentSharing as a verb to represent the action of "sharing your success to motivate your employees and get results!"

IncentShare: Both Verb and Noun

Regardless, verb or noun, IncentShare exists to help you create both short-term and long-term winning outcomes for all your stakeholders! This book was written to help you plan, design, and implement success-sharing plans for all or part of your organization. If you are in the early stages and just considering an IncentShare plan, that's fine. Use this book to help you assess the pros, cons, and considerations as you make a decision. If you already have a plan or plans in place, IncentShare can help you assess its (their) effectiveness, offer comparisons to other benchmark plans, and provide alternate ideas or improvements. If you have plans in development and need some help, you can visit IncentShare.com for other resources and ways we can assist you. Whatever your situation, we are eager to help you and your organization succeed.

IncentSharing =
Win : Win : Win : Win for
Organizations : Work groups : Employees : Others

Part 1:
Crisis in the Workplace

One cannot hire a hand;
the whole man
always comes with it.

Peter Drucker - consultant, educator, author

Engagement

Employment and engagement data differ widely. With recent unemployment data in the mid-single digits (currently under 5%, according to the Department of Labor), it would be tempting to believe that all is well in today's workplaces. But this high-profile data only reveals one aspect of employment in America. Yes, employment is in relatively positive territory, but other data reveal that employee "engagement" is shockingly low.

Most Workers Are Not Connected to Their Work.

Engagement measures are designed to quantify employee involvement and enthusiasm as well as commitment to their work, coworkers, and employer. According to experts and 2016 tracking data at Gallup, *less than one-third of employees in the United States are engaged!*[6] Of some consolation to residents of the United States, measures are far worse elsewhere, outside our country, where only 13% of employees who work for organizations are considered to be engaged.

Shockingly, Gallup data from 2014 indicated that 17.5% of employees were "actively disengaged."[7] This means that some of the individuals you believe are now working for you may actually be updating their resume, shopping online, ordering a latte for pickup, or simply daydreaming. Further per Gallup, millennials measure only 29% engaged.[8] This key group, soon to dominate the workforce and very likely vital to your future, currently makes up 38% of the US workforce, with some estimates they will comprise as much as 75% by 2025. Bottom line: while your employees may be *at* work physically, there is evidence that most are not *into* their work mentally.

Why engagement matters? Engagement is an essential strategy to enhance your workplace environment and results. Healthy work environments are increasingly relevant because they allow you to recruit, hire, motivate, and retain the best talent. Talent is a resource that can rise above all others to determine your success. Talent untapped, however, can doom you to failure. All of my research and experience indicates that true talent wants true engagement. Talented individuals want more than participation; they want to contribute to the planning, preparation, implementation, and rewards of the enterprise. Like a gifted and confident athlete, they want to "carry the ball" and "enjoy the victories." Engaged employees understand the importance of results, and they are committed to achieving them. They don't lean into these challenges blindly but rather with a heightened sense of ownership and passion. At the highest levels, talented and committed employees rise above self, realizing that teamwork and synergy allow them to accomplish greater objectives together than would be possible to achieve alone.

Engage by sharing. Increasingly, employers are considering incentives as a way to motivate their teams to boost results. Few engagement approaches are as powerful as "sharing your success" with contributing team members. Incentives help you tap into the enormous potential and underused capacity of your employees. Find a way to share success where your team benefits proportionally to the gains or improvements they make, and you will unleash employee potential like you never before imagined. Well-structured incentive plans honor all employees, respect their roles, appreciate their efforts, and reward their contributions. Sharing is a way to more closely link employees to each other and to the organization's performance. When success is shared, effort, teamwork, productivity, and more can rise significantly, resulting in better outcomes and prosperity for all stakeholders.

Leaders, don't naively assume that *employment* equals *engagement*. Realize that engagement may be the simplest way to unleash individual talent and collective teamwork. Be deliberate about connecting with your workforce, listening to its members' feedback, and integrating their input each day. Provide healthy environments within which your team can do the great work they desire. Know that much of what employees want costs less than you realize financially but more than you may be investing relationally. Share your success with incentives to focus team effort and lift motivation. Why settle for everyday employment, employees, and results when you can achieve exceptional prosperity through empowerment, encouragement, and engagement?

What Is the Level of Engagement in Your Workplace?

Check your engagement indicators. You may need to increase your sensitivity and develop methods to measure engagement in your workplace. There are multiple ways to quantify the involvement, enthusiasm, and commitment of your employees. Keep in mind both hard and soft indicators such as the following:

1. Retention
2. One-to-one feedback
3. Employee surveys
4. Performance results
5. Benchmark comparisons

"Goodbye!" One top-line engagement indicator is employee retention. How many have resigned or departed against your wishes? If you have suffered the ultimate employee *disengagement* by losing valuable talent, be sure to learn why. Schedule an exit interview before his or her departure and encourage transparent feedback. It may seem risky or awkward to have a lengthy discussion with an employee who has decided to move on, but consider the unique opportunity to get open and frank input. Certainly, keep the conversation professional and stay disciplined to avoid elevated emotions or judgment. Be ready to gain insight that would otherwise have gone unspoken or was deemed too risky to share before. When valuable employees leave, before you say goodbye, seek knowledge from which you can identify opportunities for positive workplace improvements and workforce engagement.

Sadly, I have personally had some of the most open and valuable discussions with employees on their way "out the door." Only then were they comfortable or motivated enough to share their true feelings or suggestions. Not good. Shame on me as a young leader. Realizing the value of exit interviews, I continued to schedule them for departing employees. But more importantly, I committed to find ways to keep them to a minimum.

When Did You Last Lose a Key Employee?

One-to-one meetings. Wouldn't it be better to minimize or eliminate exit interviews altogether by scheduling regular one-to-one meetings with employees *before* they depart? Use these connection opportunities to communicate, build relationships, and understand mutual wants, needs, and expectations. Consider holding one-to-ones in a comfortable environment—likely not the boss's office—that is public but allows for private conversation like a conference room or shared meeting space. Select a meeting frequency that allows for optimal connection and communication based on individual circumstances. For many employees, a good frequency is somewhere between weekly and monthly.

One benefit I personally enjoyed by having regular one-to-one meetings was the ability to *eliminate annual performance reviews.* In place of these awkward, and often ineffective, annual events, I found that regular one-to-one meetings and well-structured sharing plans, which you will learn more about in the coming pages, allowed for better communication, stronger relationships, and greater commitment to the overall success of the organization and the team.

Just ask. Employee surveys are another relatively simple and effective way to solicit worker feedback. Well-structured surveys with ten to twenty questions that take no longer than fifteen minutes to complete can produce rich input from your team in a very efficient way. Select your questions carefully and word them with nonassumptive and nonthreatening language. Use a mix of open-ended and "how would you rank" or "how would you rate" questions. Ideally, ask each person in the organization—or possibly by work group—the same questions, in the same way, at the same time, and with the same options for answers or feedback. Many employee surveys are available or can be created using online programs like SurveyMonkey.com. One well-established employee feedback resource is the Best Places to Work survey and awards program sponsored by the Best Companies Group, available in many states and regions nationwide. The program is typically administered annually and offers a well-structured employee survey that also provides comparison and benchmark data for your reference. (See also bestcompaniesgroup.com.)

Keep score. Some of my favorite employee engagement indicators are work group performance and output metrics. These measure how your most relevant results compare to your inputs of labor, time, expense, and other resources. Examples of performance indicators would be your sales or profit per employee. Output indicators might include production units (widgets) or productivity (revenue) per labor hour.

Who can you benchmark? Finally, if you can identify benchmark organizations that enjoy high levels of engagement, either within or outside your industry, you can gain a valuable reference. With benchmark comparison data, such as retention rates, morale ratings, and revenue or profit per employee, you will have a better sense of how much or how little you have to gain by investing in engagement strategies.

What to Do with Engagement Feedback

As your employees reveal their level of and desire for engagement, will you know how to respond? Don't let their input fall on deaf ears. Listen to their concerns, merge them with your organization's objectives, and commit to finding ways to achieve win-win outcomes. Include your work group leaders in the process and encourage collaboration. Engagement is significantly dependent on your leaders and their day-to-day connection with peers, team members, clients, and other stakeholders. Train them to develop their communication, coaching, and leadership skills. Emphasize that engagement is an ongoing process rather than an occasional event.

Most employees want to do great work in a healthy environment. After years of experience and leadership roles in various business, nonprofit, and volunteer organizations, I believe most employees genuinely want to do *great work* and their *personal best*. Often, they get to. Sadly, when they do not it's usually due to unhealthy or weak leadership, strategy, or processes in the work group or organization. It's easy for leaders to lose connection, leaving their workforce feeling unheard, disrespected, and unappreciated. But it's just as easy to *not* let this happen.

What Employees Want, Need, and Expect

A simple list, years in the making. I compiled the list below of employee wants, needs, and expectations over more than twenty-five years. As a young leader, I quickly learned how important it was to meet or exceed the expectations of my coworkers. Thankfully, as my awareness, knowledge, and fulfillment of employees' wants and needs grew, so did my effectiveness. For me, it was a maturing process. As I became more mindful of others, relationships that were once challenging began to improve. Many issues that had lingered before, often because I failed to understand another person's perspective, gradually got resolved.

Leaders, consider how much better you could serve your organization—and yourself—by being mindful of these employee needs, wants, and expectations:

Purpose
Respect and Appreciation
Connection and Belonging
Clear Expectations
Structure and Organization
Safety, Security, and Stability
Compensation and Benefits
Training and Development
Career Opportunities
Freedom and Flexibility
Fun

To me, the list above is fundamentally about leadership and re-lationships. It generally flows in sequential order from the top down. I must admit that some of the practices on the list I've been able to adopt and provide easily, while others continue to challenge and elude me.

The needs, wants, and expectations above are not exclusive to *employees* and could justifiably be broadened to include *all* others. I consider the list a gift shared and taught to me by mentors, coworkers, family, friends, and through my faith. Each day I find wisdom and guidance in it as I strive to manage my relationships as a husband, father, friend, volunteer, and leader. Perhaps you will as well.

"A Guide for Leaders"

Employees Need, Want, and Expect:

Purpose
Respect
Appreciation
Connection
Belonging
Clear Expectations
Structure
Organization
Safety
Security
Stability
Compensation
Benefits
Training
Development
Career Opportunities
Freedom
Flexibility
Fun

*Many hands
make light work.*

John Heywood - English writer, playwright

Why Do We Work?

152,000,000 Workers. As of this writing, there are about 325 million people living in the United States, including men, women, and children. The Department of Labor indicates about 152 million are employed.[9] Another eight million or so are unemployed but desiring work, and about 2.4 million of them entered the unemployment ranks in just the past five weeks. The Bureau of Labor Statistics further indicates that all employees on private, nonfarm payrolls worked, on average, 34.4 hours per week.[10] The median weekly earnings for the nation's 112.8 million *full-time* wage and salary workers was $827 in the most recent calendar quarter.[11]

The data above confirms that an enormous number of people, hours, and dollars are linked to *work* being done by *workers* in various *workplaces*. The stakes and impact are quite high.

So why do we work? The answer may seem obvious, but upon reflection we realize that there are truly many reasons why people choose employment.

Why work? Author Barry Schwartz, in his book *Why We Work*, asks this crucial question and offers an interesting perspective on why people drag themselves out of bed each morning instead of living lives composed of one pleasure-filled adventure after another.[12]

Mr. Schwartz acknowledges that we work because we have to make a living but then asks the question *is that it?* Of course not, he states. The author proceeds to explore work *fulfillment* beyond a paycheck and what provides *satisfaction.* Satisfied workers are engaged by their work, losing themselves in it most or much of the time. Satisfied workers are challenged by their work. It forces them to stretch themselves and go outside their comfort zones. Satisfied people do their work because they feel they are in charge and their workday offers them a degree of autonomy and discretion. They use that autonomy and discretion to achieve a level of mastery or expertise as they learn new things to develop both as workers and as people. Satisfied employees find meaning in their work and an opportunity to make a difference in the world and thereby make other people's lives better. Mr. Schwartz declares that we wouldn't work if we didn't get paid, but that's not at the core of why we do what we do. The most fulfilled workers work for the satisfaction that it provides.

Why We Work broadens the perspective of work and shares some interesting nonmonetary reasons why many of us enter the weekday "commuter caravan." I must admit, however, that I differ with the author, a professor of psychology with forty-five years in academia according to his LinkedIn profile, when he generally dismisses the importance of earnings and income as integral to work satisfaction. On the one hand he acknowledges that *we work because we have to make a living,* but then goes on to disregard earnings as an almost insignificant element of job satisfaction and engagement. Professor Schwartz declares that "money almost never comes up" when fulfilled workers are asked why they do the work they do; however, their list of nonmonetary reasons for working is "long and compelling." Has that been *your* experience as a business or organization leader?

While I agree with the importance of fulfillment and nonmonetary work satisfaction, my experience is that the benefits, security, challenge, satisfaction, and freedom provided by financial rewards—and especially incentives—can be equally fulfilling. For most people throughout the world, workplace *earnings* provide food, shelter, and clothing at a minimum and at best provide healthcare, education, savings, travel, leisure, charity, entrepreneurship, and much more. Hardly insignificant, and in my opinion, *financial* success-sharing offers an enormous opportunity for many organizations.

The Spirit of Competition and Teamwork

Are you among team players? In what activities or sports have you participated as a member, player, coach, leader, or other contributor? What's the best team you've ever been a part of? Have you experienced the adrenaline produced by competition that brought out your best? Have you enjoyed team camaraderie and the resulting lift in your team's capabilities as you worked and practiced together and then entered fields-of-play to outperform an opponent? From backyard games and grade-school athletics on up to college and professional sports, there is significant motivation that comes from high levels of competition and working together as a team. Unfortunately, most workplaces never achieve this level of team spirit and its corresponding benefits. Why is this so? *If only* the "spirit of competition and teamwork" was sufficient to motivate your team at work!

In a Workplace, Teamwork Is More Complicated.

Do you realize that many in the workplace have *never* formally participated on a team? According to 2008 data from the US Census Bureau, only 35% of children between six and seventeen years participated in after-school sports, and 43% did *not participate in any* after-school extracurricular activity including athletics, clubs, or lessons like music, dance, or language.[13] People in this group, likely representative of your employees, may never have benefited from the excitement of competition, thrill of victory, anguish of loss, and the many lessons these experiences bring. Expecting your workforce to have an innate desire to perform, cooperate, compete, and "win" as a team is unrealistic in most workplaces.

The *primary reason why most people choose to be employed is to provide* for the needs of their families and themselves. Certainly, each person's motives are varied and weighted differently, but at the core is a powerful essential need for "provision" through compensation and benefits.

Provision (Compensation and Benefits) Is the Core Reason Why Most People Choose to Be Employed.

Anything we do as leaders in a workplace to address employee motivation—apart from fundamental provision—may be overlooking the obvious. Properly structured IncentShare plans link the core provisional needs of employees to the critical outcomes of the organization. The IncentShare premise is that employee provision increases in some proportion to improved organizational results.

What About Noncompensation Approaches to Motivate?

Is it all about the money? No. The point here is not to diminish the value of noncompensation approaches to motivate. In fact, there are typically great advantages to using smart noncompensation motivation strategies and tactics. For example, pep talks, recognition events, awards, celebrations, gifts, and parties could be low-cost or no-cost approaches to lift your employee's spirits and enthusiasm. Use them! Just realize the limitations and potential risk of these methods, especially as they grow in cost, time-expended, or your expectation of them relative to other approaches.

As you use motivation strategies and tactics apart from compensation, carefully monitor the time, money, staff hours, and return for your investment. Here's one example why:

The Year-End Celebration that Underdelivers

Flop. It's not uncommon for some organizations to spend many hours and thousands of dollars in preparation for a year-end celebration or holiday party that ends up being awkward and mostly unappreciated. Too often, these events are created as or evolve into self-serving events for the organization, event-planning staff, or owners. Many times these gatherings make the guests so uncomfortable that the return on investment goes sadly negative, especially given the time and money expended. The point here is not to kill the year-end party but instead to encourage you to consider *why* you hold these events and *what* you should reasonably expect to accomplish with them. Yes, celebrate your wins, accomplishments, and seasons, but be careful to keep the focus on the team and not expect these occasional events to carry your team's morale and motivation by themselves.

Rely First on What May Be the Most Effective and Lowest-Cost Motivator: Share Ongoing Respect, Appreciation, and Encouragement!

Perhaps your first motivation approach—and certainly the most cost effective—should be to show ongoing and genuine respect, appreciation, and encouragement to individuals and teams! Much of this can occur in the daily connections and communication between you and your employees. Don't overlook the power of your words when spoken and captured in writing through e-mail, letters, and your correspondence with others. As you move forward, why not make the most of this simple and hopefully obvious starting point to motivate your organization?

"

Give, and it will be given to you. Good measure, pressed down, shaken together, running over, will be put into your lap. For with the measure you use it will be measured back to you.

"

Luke 6:38 ESV

The Employee Dilemma

How Many Relational Groups are Tugging at Your Employees?

Competing interests. Your workforce is burdened with a dilemma. The dilemma is "competing relational interests," and it exists in virtually every organization. Even in a small workplace with just a few employees, individuals must develop and sustain multiple professional and personal relationships. Have you considered the challenge this presents to your employees and for you as an employer?

Your employees are relationally challenged. A typical employee has a unique relationship with his or her supervisor and each of his or her peers and direct reports. Many employees also have professional relationships with customers, resellers, suppliers, vendors, community partners, and others. Depending on the size of your organization, there could be dozens or hundreds of internal and external relationships with individuals, groups, and various stakeholders that are linked in some way to your enterprise.

Beyond the organization, many employees must also navigate relationships at home with a significant other, spouse, children, family members, and friends. You can be certain that effectively managing multiple relationships *is a challenge* for even your most relationally gifted employees!

Tally the numbers. How many individuals would you or your coworkers list in each of the relational groups below?

Consider and Quantify These Relational Groups:

_____ Family
_____ Owners
_____ Investors
_____ Supervisors
_____ Peers
_____ Direct Reports
_____ Customers
_____ Resellers
_____ Distributors

_____ Suppliers
_____ Vendors
_____ Sub-contractors
_____ Community
_____ Other Groups

Pulled in different directions. As individuals are tugged or swayed by others, their loyalties can become divided, distracted, and diluted. For many employees, their weakest and most at-risk relationship is with you, their employer, or the organization at large. Too often, connection and loyalty to the organization drifts to the bottom of the relational priority list, overtaken by personal relationships that develop between and among peers, customers, suppliers, subordinates, supervisors, and others.

Human nature. It's easy to be swayed or negatively manipulated by others at work, especially if not motivated to behave otherwise. Consider the following circumstances:

- Managers who choose to avoid rather than confront poorly performing employees.
- Employees who let coworkers waste their time on frivolous matters, rather than risk conflict by resisting.
- Sales reps who give outside-the-original-agreement concessions to customers who are pushy or difficult, or are alternatively overly friendly or manipulative.
- Purchasers who avoid shopping, choosing instead to pay top dollar to smooth-talking or gift-giving company vendors.
- Shop workers who keep their head down and stay quiet rather than challenge wasteful peers or practices.

- Optimistic leaders who avoid making critical changes for a week, month, or year longer than was obvious to others.
- Coworkers who overlook the lazy or less-than-desirable work habits of some peers, believing they have no say.
- Family members of owners who take advantage of time, payroll, policies, personnel, and more.
- Remote workers who use time and resources poorly while seemingly out of sight and out of mind.
- Discouraged innovators who avoid the risk or defeat of suggestions, having been shut down or told "no" too many times.

Yikes. If biased or manipulated personal relationships in your workplace result in a diminished focus on organizational outcomes, performance will certainly suffer. For the enterprise to prosper, the commitment and loyalty of each employee to the organization must be *at or near the top* of all their relationships. Accomplishing this isn't easy, but it's worth the effort that may be required. Leaders, be aware of these relational dynamics as you work to establish and strengthen each employee's connection and loyalty to the collective organization. One powerful solution is to create a cooperative environment and teamwork culture where *every employee benefits most by working together* for the success of the company or business.

Committed and Loyal to What?

To whom or to what are your employees most loyal? Right now, how committed are your employees to your organization relative to their peers, customers, suppliers, supervisors, direct reports, families, and others? Don't be surprised that their loyalties may be divided or significantly swayed by individuals or groups. What's the level of teamwork within and between work groups? To what extent are your employees selfish, putting *me* ahead of *we*?

Sometimes Leaders Unwittingly Promote or Passively Enable Selfish Behaviors through Their Own Weak Leadership.

Consider how dependent you are on your leaders or supervisors who work on the relational front lines with your employees. Do you appropriately recognize and monitor these relationships? How strong are the connections between supervisors and their work group and peers, and where do they stand relative to *other* competing relational interests? If your supervisors are the "face of your organization," do they represent your organization as you would like? Leadership training could be a worthwhile investment for these supervisors. One goal would be for your employees to say their *best* (professional) relationship is between them and their supervisor. Would your supervisor and work-group members say that about you?

Strengthen the relationship with your organization by sharing your success. Few things unite and focus a team more than a common objective that, if achieved, will benefit everyone. Smart incentive plans, directly linked to success measures for each work group, are a powerful way to unite employees and motivate them to perform their best for the benefit of the organization as well as their peers, families, and themselves. Compensation or rewards that are proportional to team success can give individuals much greater reason to communicate, stay focused, work together, innovate, and overcome obstacles. Competing relational interests decline when organization and work-group objectives are clearly defined and linked to employee rewards and benefits.

Overcome the relational dilemma. Give your employees reason to have their most committed nonfamily relationship with your *organization* by directly linking their compensation and rewards to its outcomes and success!

"

Hire people who are better than you are, then leave them to get on with it. Look for people who will aim for the remarkable, who will not settle for the routine.

"

David Ogilvy - advertising pioneer

The World Has Changed

Leaders, how well are you keeping up? Many of today's seasoned leaders started their careers or their companies one, two, or even three decades ago. Perhaps this is you. If you have memories from the previous millennium, it's critical that you merge your lessons learned in the past with the new realities of today's workplace and workforce. Many of the circumstances and situations that existed in your "formative leadership years" have obviously changed. How well have you kept up? What's your strategy to stay current?

Take a look at the chart by decade on the next page. How far back do you remember? Which time period affected you most? What was most relevant for you in each decade with regard to society, technology, the workplace, and organizations you knew and admired? To be successful, you must keep up with today's world and workplace. The following seemed most relevant to me as I read about, researched, or lived through the following decades.[14]

The 1960s

Society	Kennedy, Vietnam, Woodstock, Beatles, Martin Luther King, James Bond, Wilt Chamberlain
Technology	Transistors, space race, moon landing, nuclear power, vinyl records, Teflon, film cameras, eight tracks
Organizations	Kodak, Sears, Kmart, JC Penney, ABC, NBC, Gulf, Esso, Boeing, GE, GM, Ford, poor-quality imports
Workplace	Loyal, trusted, stable, pensions, job for life, work local, buy local, neighborhood retailers

The 1970s

Society	Nixon, Watergate, M*A*S*H, test-tube baby, cold war, Carter, gas lines, disco, the Fonz, Johnny Carson
Technology	Calculators, Pong, Three Mile Island, computer tape, cassettes, synthesizers, Tang
Organizations	Xerox, Pan Am, DeLorean, American Motors, Woolworth's, Westinghouse, Disney World, Nike, Datsun
Workplace	Job security, big and stable, quality, electric typewriters, inflation, working women, phone booths, retail malls

The 1980s

Society	Reagan, Apple Macintosh, Berlin Wall, MTV, Tiananmen Square, Michael Jackson, Madonna, yuppies, AIDS
Technology	Microsoft, dot matrix printers, floppy discs, Pac-Man, CNN, microwave oven, VCRs, space shuttle, Fax
Organizations	Compaq, Intel, TI, Dell, Microsoft, FedEx, CNN, HBO, Honda, Eastern Air Lines, RCA, ESPN, Walmart
Workplace	PCs, Lotus123, word processing, Excellence, 401(k), 800#s, direct deposit, ATMs, Chernobyl, Exxon Valdez

The 1990s

Society	Bush, Desert Storm, Princess Diana, Clinton, Mandela, Michael Jordan, Toy Story, sushi, mutual funds
Technology	Portable phones, videotapes, Hubble Telescope, cable channels, DVDs, caller ID, computer automation
Organizations	HP, AOL, Pixar, Sony, Fox TV, USA Today, Domino's, QVC; Samsung, Toyota, Blockbuster, TWA, Enron
Workplace	World Wide Web, Windows, video learning, robots, shop from TV, home delivery, Six Sigma, Monster.com

The 2000s

Society	Bush, 9/11/2001, Iraq War, Katrina, *American Idol*, Tiger Woods, Michael Phelps, SUVs, *Survivor*, PlayStation
Technology	Y2K, Internet, GPS, human genome, CDs, memory sticks, broadband, cheap memory, digital cameras, iPods
Organizations	Microsoft, Apple, HP, Starbucks, Home Depot, Blackberry, Myspace, YouTube, Pets.com, China's emergence
Workplace	2000 tech bubble, Monster.com, work-from-home, smoke-free, LEAN, 2008 recession, wind energy

The 2010s

Society	Obama, war on terror, social media, shootings, *The Voice*, microbrews, ETFs, fracked energy, big data, Trump
Technology	Smartphones, HDTV, Kindle, LED lighting, 3D printing, drones, cloud computing, Li ion, AI, mobile apps
Organizations	Facebook, Amazon, Netflix, Google, Tesla, Yuengling, Uber, Chipotle, Glassdoor, *Shark Tank* start-ups
Workplace	Shared workspace, multiple careers, online learning, Indeed.com, freelancers, SEO, AdWords, free info

The 2020s

Society	Healthier lives with many options, more complexity and faster change, more experiences, smaller homes
Technology	Medical advances, globalization, Internet of things, electric self-driving vehicles, off-grid power, space, Mars
Organizations	Mega companies and countries along with micro enterprises that stay relevant changing the world
Workplace	Work from anywhere, free agents, many careers, work-play-fun merge, work-life balance, IncentSharing

The 2030s+

Society	Big gains to world health, poverty reduction, communication and peace, greater abundance and prosperity for all
Technology	Advances in health, communication, energy, and transportation benefiting many more for much less
Organizations	Amazing global contributions from new and fast-rising participants in places like India, South America, and Africa
Workplace	Abundant information and opportunities letting individuals everywhere self-train, work, contribute, and prosper

Relevance is key if you want to remain an effective leader. You may find it helpful to consider how society, technology, and the workplace have changed over the past few decades. Does history just simply repeat itself, or will you face a wild, wacky, or wonderful world ahead? Likely, you will experience some of both. A brief look at decades past and a decade or so ahead may help you remember what was, accept more of what is, and anticipate some of what may become relevant so you can remain sharp as a leader.

How is your team performing? Are you doing what it takes to recruit, motivate, and retain the talent necessary to succeed today? It's important to consider what level of talent you need for each role in your business. It's equally important to understand what you must offer as an employer to entice and retain the best players on your team. The good news is there have never been more resources available to help you to learn about and understand who's winning the workplace game for talent and how. Websites like Indeed.com, LinkedIn.com, CareerBuilder.com, Craigslist.com, and others give you almost unlimited access to the tactics and job offerings of employers large and small.

Online insights. One relatively new website, Glassdoor.com, offers unique information not easily found elsewhere. Glassdoor claims to be among the fastest-growing job and recruiting websites.[15] Its mission is to "help people everywhere find jobs and companies they love." How do they do this? Well, for one by soliciting information from over thirty million users who share not only feedback about their current and former employers but also compensation and benefit details.

At Glassdoor you can access over eight million company reviews to learn what *employees have shared* and are saying about jobs and employers, sometimes in contrast to the polished presentation put out by company leadership or PR spin masters. Of particular interest on Glassdoor are the Best Places to Work benchmark organizations, CEO ratings, and benefit and compensation data that includes low, high, and average earnings by job and by company. In exchange for this information, the site asks users to share their own data and experience for the benefit of others. Welcome to the world of free, open, and shared information that simply couldn't be found a decade ago.

Are you doing your research? When did you last update your company's online profiles? You can be sure that the best workforce candidates know where to look for job and workplace insights. Just assume that *they* have done their homework and will arrive at your interview with powerful knowledge and sharpened negotiating skills. Are you ready for them?

Welders and Walmart Managers

Two examples. Consider two jobs that you would find in a typical midsized town in America: a welder and a Walmart manager. While you might think these jobs are oddly chosen and different, you may be surprised at the similar career opportunities they afford to those who fill them.

Welders cut, shape, and join various materials such as steel and aluminum. The next time you go in, under, or over a structure, there's a good chance you can thank a welder for making it possible. Although welding was developed over one hundred years ago, this specialized skill is still in strong demand today. The US Bureau of Labor Statistics (BLS) claims that in 2014 there were over 397,900 welding jobs and they are expected to grow by 4% per year.[16] According to the BLS, "welders with up-to-date training should have good job opportunities." It's not surprising that *billboards* in my hometown are currently advertising opportunities for...welders! Glassdoor.com currently lists over 4,500 welding jobs available across the United States. The 2015 median pay for welders nationally was $18.34 per hour and $38,150 per year.[17] According to submissions on Glassdoor, gathered from over 1,100 welders, their salaries can range from a low of $25,000 to a high of $55,000 nationally. Several welding jobs recently listed on the site were at or above $55,000, which reinforces this data. And these compensation figures do not include additional workplace training and benefits generously offered by many mid- to large-size employers. In addition, many companies offer flexible work schedules—four ten-hour days per week for example—and the opportunity for overtime hours and pay. Not too bad for an occupation that often requires no related work experience, and the typical entry level education is a high-school diploma.

Let's head over to Walmart. The $480-plus-billion-dollar retail conglomerate—WMT is number one on the 2016 *Fortune 500* list—is likely to have one of its multiple-format stores just a few miles from where you are now sitting.[18] No stranger to employment controversy, Walmart has worked hard to shrug off its employee-unfriendly reputation. In fact, Walmart is a huge employer that provides over 2,300,000 jobs to associates worldwide. All of these employees are needed to service a mind-boggling 260,000,000 customer experiences *each week*. These days, not all of those are in traditional stores. According to an online report by *Forbes* in May of 2016, Walmart is currently number two in Internet sales but a good distance behind Amazon, the leading online retailer.

Anticipating growth and clearly recognizing the need for fresh and rising talent, Walmart offers the following perspective on employees and hiring: "Walmart's success is dependent upon engaged, motivated associates who love serving customers. Globally, we are doing more to invest in our associates' futures—through increased training and development, higher pay, and better opportunities to build rewarding careers. Walmart is positioned to win the future of retail by providing a ladder of opportunity for every member of our team." Powerful words, but how will they deliver?

Glassdoor.com offers one perspective of how Walmart is attracting and rewarding talent. Submissions on Glassdoor by over 1,000 *cashiers and sales associates* reveal that Walmart pays from a low of around $7 up to a high about $17 per hour nationally ($9.25 on average) for employees who fill these roles.[19] Additional submissions from over 250 *assistant managers* indicate that Walmart's base compensation for this category of employee ranges from $36,000 to $66,000. Some of these managers report additional cash or stock bonuses and *profit sharing* that can add up an additional $40,000 or more annually. Assistants who are promoted to *store managers* at Walmart can earn from $88,000 to $240,000 in total compensation with the reported average over $150,000, according to Glassdoor.

In addition to compensation, Walmart offers competitive benefits that include store discounts, matching 401(k) contributions up to 6%, health and disability insurance, paid time off, training, and more.

Are you keeping up? The world, workforce, and workplace keep changing. Don't be left behind by yesterday's information or practices. Stay smart by investing time online, with your current employees, with prospective employees, and with other employers to stay current with new and changing workplace practices.

Identify benchmark companies to follow and learn from. Where possible, connect with their leaders, visit their facilities, read their annual reports, and follow their news feeds.

To succeed, you must develop a team of talented individuals. But it's no easy task in a fast-changing world because the best talent is more knowledgeable, in more control, and in greater demand by the best organizations that are eager to find top performers for critical roles like welders and Walmart managers.

Part 2:
Are Incentives and Sharing Right for You?

*I don't pay good wages
because I have a lot of money;
I have a lot of money because
I pay good wages.*

Robert Bosch - founder of Bosch GmbH

Eight Questions to Consider

How to Decide
if Incentives and Sharing Are Right for You?

Adding or enhancing a variable compensation plan is a big decision. The following questions will help you determine if incentives or sharing based on performance are right for your organization.

Question #1
How Big Is Your Opportunity?

How large is the gap between your organization's potential and its current results? How much room do you have to improve and grow? Compared to your peers and best-in-class competitors, how are you performing? Assessing your potential and how much is "at stake" will help you decide how much time and effort to invest in incentives as a performance-enhancing strategy. Imagine how a 10% improvement in sales, margins, productivity, waste reduction, new customers, expense savings, or profitability would impact your business.

It's important to recognize the strategies that will help you get there as well as how dependent the success of those strategies will be on the focus, effort, and teamwork of your employees. Would "rewarding performance" impact the outcomes of your improvement strategies, and if so by how much?

You May Have Massive Room for Improvement.

What is the mind-set in your organization? Do most believe that you are just getting started, the future is exciting, and your best times are ahead? Or, do some employees feel that all is fine, we're pretty good, we can't get much better, there's little more to accomplish so therefore keep our heads down, don't rock the boat, why make waves, or let's just drift?

Are You Sprinting or Toddling?

If you are at or near the peak of your potential, then it may take a great deal to squeeze out just marginal improvement. Usain Bolt, known as "the fastest human ever," regularly clocks well under ten seconds for a 100-meter run. Bolt set, and still currently holds, the world record at 9.58 seconds for 100 meters in 2009.[20] For Usain "Lightning" Bolt, improvement is measured in hundredths of a second, and each one-hundredth requires hundreds of hours to train and prepare.

On the other extreme of human performance, think of a one-year-old toddler. Just a few steps across the room is a worthy achievement but consider the improvement to come! Take a moment to think about where your organization's performance falls in the range from unsteady toddler to world-class sprinter. What will it take to move it steadily forward?

Quantify Your Opportunities.

Consider the value of opportunities gained or opportunities lost. Identify your most important outcomes and quantify what different levels of achievement would be worth. Start with just a 10% improvement, then go on to consider the value of bigger (two-, five-, ten-times) potential gains. Are your opportunities valued in the ten thousands, hundreds of thousands, or even millions? When you quantify your opportunities, you will more clearly see the path to capture them.

Question #2
How Engaged and Motivated Is Your Workforce?

\ Think about why people do the things they do at home or work. Consider the motivations behind their behaviors. For good or for bad, our motivations influence our attitudes, decisions, actions, habits, effort, and engagement.

A Recent Gallup Survey Revealed that Less Than One-Third (31.5%) of US Workers Were Engaged in Their Jobs and 17.5% Were "Actively Disengaged"

As a business owner, executive, or team leader, you can't bypass motivation. You have to embrace and leverage it. One of the most powerful ways to leverage motivation is through incentives.

In a workplace setting, a well-structured incentive plan can significantly increase, even double, organizational performance, but not just in the ways you might expect. Consider these benefits that many experience after sharing the success of their organization with variable compensation linked to performance:

Potential Benefits of Incentives:

Better Communication
Increased Focus

Greater Teamwork
Improved Productivity
Employee Retention
Talent Recruitment
Innovation
Entrepreneurship

Most of us don't show up and automatically perform at our best. For various reasons often linked to motivation, we fall short as individuals and as teams. When examining our potential, we must accept the realities of motivation and how to extract the very best from ourselves and our workforce.

Think about how rewarding performance might impact the likelihood of your team nearing its potential and the speed at which it improves. Incentives could be the way to leverage the motivation, pace, and performance of your workforce.

Question #3
How Do You Define Success?

It's important to identify what success looks like for your organization. Think about the hard and soft measures you use to decide if you are performing well or not. How you define and quantify success is critical as you prepare for the future, develop strategies to improve, implement your plans, and then measure your results to confirm that your approaches are working.

Successful leaders and compensation experts know that the best sharing plans are linked to specific and measurable results. Identifying what outcomes best indicate your success is a key step as you develop sharing plans.

You may find several if not dozens of indicators to consider measuring. Work to prioritize these indicators and decide how the results will be quantified. You will also need to determine how to report the results and who will have access to this data.

The following are some categories to consider as you determine the best success indicators:

Success Indicator Categories:

1. Risk Management
2. Stakeholder Satisfaction
3. Financial Results
4. Productivity Improvement
5. Growth
6. Personal Development

Whatever your success indicators, you will likely find that different indicators are more relevant to one work group than another. This is typical of most organizations. We see this clearly in sports such as football, where the offense, defense, and special teams each makes a unique contribution to the team and uses different indicators to measure success. Businesses and organizations are no different. What measurements best reveal your work group's or individual's performance? To develop effective sharing plans, it's essential to identify these.

Question #4
How Is Your Workforce Organized?

How big is your workforce, and how is it organized? How clearly have you defined roles and responsibilities both for individuals and for functional teams or work groups? What does your organizational chart look like?

Beyond the start-up entrepreneur or solo performer, organizations grow and add employees. Employees are typically hired based on how their background, education, experience, gifts, skills, and talents can help them perform specific tasks, fill roles, and assume responsibilities. How you organize and group your functional teams will be a factor when considering incentives. And don't forget the stakeholders that are sometimes outside the walls of your company.

Consider the following groups, their roles, and how they contribute to your success:

Investors
Owners
Senior Leadership
Work Group Leaders
R&D
Marketing
Field Sales
Inside Sales
Customer Service
Manufacturing
Warehouse
Shipping
Technicians
Accounting
HR
IT
Facilities
Maintenance

Sometimes sharing or incentive plans tie everyone to one company-wide plan. At other times, they link variable compensation to the unique contribution of the work group or occasionally even to individual performance. Always consider how those being incentivized are linked to the work being done. This approach could help you more effectively motivate and empower individuals and work groups.

Question #5
What Experience Have You Had with Incentives?

Some have had no exposure to incentives or sharing plans while others have extensive experience. Good or bad, what are your team's perceptions? Past experience or preconceived notions about incentives could be a significant hurdle for you. Or, it could be a tailwind!

It's important to get input from participants, especially your leaders, to address their questions, concerns, and exposure to incentives, variable compensation, and sharing. It's better to hear and respond to pros and cons up-front than to let concerns go unspoken and unaddressed. Here are some questions to ask your team:

What opportunities do you see ahead for our organization, and what is our potential?

_____

_____

_____

What is holding us back, and what would bridge the gap between current results and our potential?

_____

_____

_____

How big a factor is motivation and engagement among our workforce?

_____

_____

_____

What results might we achieve if we found a way to "share our success" with more of our team?

_____

_____

_____

What experience have you had—good or bad—with incentives or variable compensation plans?

_____

_____

_____

What concerns or questions do you have regarding sharing via incentives?

_____

_____

_____

Question #6
How Do You Compensate Now?

How do you pay your employees? What do you reward? Do you have a mix of salaried and hourly workers? Do you pay them weekly or biweekly based on a prenegotiated salary or hourly rate? Is any of their compensation variable, and if so, based on what? What percentage of compensation is earned by "hours (or days) worked" versus "business performance"? Another way of asking this is:

How Much Do You Reward Your Workforce for Time Spent versus Results Accomplished?

What is your organization's overtime experience? How many overtime (OT) hours are typically worked each week? Who usually works the overtime? Is there a "culture of overtime" where individuals or work groups expect to work OT and perhaps even see it as their best way to get ahead and provide for their families? How much are you rewarding their effort, intellect, and output versus the time they log?

Do You Have an "Overtime Culture"?

Most organizations have struggled to find the best way to compensate and reward their teams. Their owners and leaders genuinely appreciate employee effort and work done well. They want to express their gratitude and have tried various ways to do so. Sometimes, uncertainty about how to design and implement an optimal incentive plan gets in the way of their good intentions.

One approach that some organizations use is to pay a "discretionary bonus," typically at the end of the year, based on an ambiguous or loosely defined set of criteria often decided by the owner(s) of the organization. This may be better than nothing and could be much appreciated. Is this your situation?

Another approach, which has the potential for a *much* greater impact, is to carefully plan up-front (at the beginning of the year, quarter, or performance season) how the success of the organization will be determined, measured, and shared in a fair, carefully formulated, and low-risk way. It's not necessary to implement this for all people or work groups at once. It might be better to start with one work group and then extend the approach to other work groups in a progressive, methodical, and carefully implemented way over several months or quarters. Here's the essence of this change:

From: Year-End Discretionary Bonus

To: Preplanned Performance Sharing

Rewards, incentives, and sharing *do* influence motivation and behavior at organizations that use them. Consider the positive consequences of shifting your approach from no incentives or a discretionary end-of-season reward to a carefully structured plan that you communicate up-front. Consider using this approach and expanding it progressively, one work group at a time, until eventually all work groups participate and share as you succeed and grow.

Question #7
What Is Your Timing?

Why wait? Time is often underappreciated when making strategic decisions. How much is time a factor as you consider incentive or sharing plans? What is your process to assess, make a decision, and implement improvements like these, even if for just one work group? What opportunities could be captured in your sales, production, development, finance, field operations, customer care, or other work groups with a more motivated and engaged workforce? What is the "opportunity cost" to hesitate or delay a decision?

Consider using "opportunity math." If your organization has the potential to realize a million dollars of new, untapped, or hidden opportunity, that would roughly equal $20,000 per week or $4,000 per workday!

Use Opportunity Math:

$1,000,000 annual opportunity / 50 workweeks = $20,000 / workweek

$20,000 opportunity / workweek = $4,000 / workday

What are your opportunities worth over time? What is your opportunity math? What is the cost of delaying, diminishing, or defraying your organization's opportunities?

Question #8
Are You Ready to Take a Next Step?

What Are Your Questions or Concerns? Have these questions helped you decide if incentives are right for you? Did they help you appreciate the scope and potential benefits of "sharing your success" with incentives? Do you believe that well-structured and implemented plans can minimize the real or perceived risks of incentives and boost your team's motivation and outcomes? If so, read on to learn how to use sharing and incentives to *boost* your results.

If I were running a company today, I would have one priority above all others: to acquire as many of the best people as I could [because] the single biggest constraint on the success of my organization is the ability to get and to hang on to enough of the right people.

Jim Collins - author, *Good to Great*

IncentShare-Origins and Evolution

Observations of a new young leader. There was no crisis at the small rural manufacturing company. Most workers would show up every day and seem to do their job just fine. Productivity was OK. There was a general rhythm and hum about the place as various chemicals and containers came in, and packaged cleaners, lubricants, and coatings shipped out. Several large customers had been with the company for years, sending in their orders—and checks—like clock-work. Employee morale seemed fine, and no one had quit in months. The owner of the business was actively engaged but not overbearing and seemingly content. But something was missing.

I may not have cared so much about the pulse of the organization had I not been recently promoted to a new leadership position there. After a few years spent working my way through roles as a sales engineer, sales manager, and marketing manager, I had now been given the opportunity to become general manager of the small, but growing, business. I was certainly engaged. After years of working diligently and getting to know many aspects of the business, I was now given a chance to be in charge of the company, *or at least that's what I thought.*

What, Me a Motivator?

As a new young leader, it was hard to describe the personal tension I felt between excitement and fear. Excitement for the potential to learn, grow, and enjoy rewards that could come from the next level of leadership but also fear of the many unknowns and the high chance of failure. Each day was an exercise in self-control—on the one hand trying to manage the emotional highs that came with the new responsibility and influence and on the other navigating the emotional dips created by uncertainty and self-doubt. It took daily study and self-discipline to learn how to behave like a leader, develop plans to ensure that the company would not falter, and create effective and efficient processes to make life for several dozen workers a little better each day. Diligence and planning needed to replace distractions and my insecurity.

Given my interest and background in math, science, and engineering—call me a nerd, it's OK—my go-to approach had always been to use my *mind* and work *smarter* to solve problems. I felt a primary responsibility to come up with an approach or strategy to ensure the short-term survival of the business and eventually to build a foundation upon which the organization and our employees could thrive and prosper. What would it take to find a way where *all* participants could benefit from improving the company?

Empty Soda Bottles and Hot Wheels

Incentives were always intriguing to me about as far back as I can remember. As a kid, I had worked in various jobs and roles where my pay and rewards were tied directly to my effort, results, and increasingly my innovation. The earliest experience I can remember is in the first years of elementary school when my best friend and I would walk the city streets of our small, northeast Pennsylvania coal-region town, looking for empty soda bottles. At the time, these empty bottles could be returned to the local grocery store for a penny or two. They were like found treasure, at least to a six- or seven-year-old kid. Several laps around a few city blocks were sure to bring in 5–10 cents, enough for a nice reward: a vanilla popsicle. As I look back, I have to thank my mom and dad for allowing me to scrounge the neighborhood surprisingly unsupervised but certainly motivated to learn a life-changing lesson about results and rewards.

My early education about effort and performance continued. When possible, I would negotiate with a relative or neighbor to do chores, run an errand, or otherwise earn nickels or dimes. This bounty was promptly placed in my equivalent of Fort Knox, a small metal Sucrets container with a tiny metal hinge and clasp. I enjoyed saving my earnings and watching my little container get increasingly full, with one exception. The exception I would make was to dip into my savings to buy Hot Wheels, the newest and hottest toys to hit the (under 42-inch, youth) market. Because I rarely had enough money to buy new Hot Wheels, I most often would barter, trade, and negotiate for less-expensive, used vehicles on the open (cafeteria and schoolyard) market.

Fast-Forward about Thirty-Five Years

Little did I know that my childhood interests and activities were tiny seeds that would bear bigger fruit than I could have imagined.

My youthful passion for innovative work, negotiation, sales, marketing, and automobiles established a foundation that would later allow me to become a senior executive (CEO) of a world-class manufacturing company that marketed and sold car care products worldwide to the largest automotive distributors and retailers. (See also www.InvisibleGlass.com and www.StonerSolutions.com.) For years, this work took me regularly to the largest international auto shows and racing venues as well as into the negotiation rooms of the biggest and most successful international businesses like AutoZone, Advance Auto, PepBoys, O'Reilly Automotive, Walmart, Target, Home Depot, Lowes, Dollar General, True Value, Meijer, Menards, QVC, and more.

Looking back to my days as a young leader, I was very eager—at times desperate—to find innovative ways to help our business succeed. I soon realized that success was indeed a prerequisite for keeping my job. There were numerous ideas and strategies that we considered. Our general approach was to learn wherever we could and seek out benchmark performers where possible. Often, we would learn good ideas and find inspiration and encouragement from leading organizations that were "pioneering" best practices and achieving significantly better results. Continuous learning, testing, and benchmarking became an integral part of our culture.[21]

Parking Lot Insight

A strategic breakthrough in—of all places—the parking lot. I often worked late into the evening, but on this day I was leaving the office around 5:00 p.m. at the end of our official workday. In the parking lot I met a coworker, one of our midlevel leaders named Jerry who was on his way out the door, headed for home. The brief, but very interesting, stand-up conversation we had was an eye-opener. Our discussion rocked me not just for what Jerry said but even more for what it implied. Jerry mentioned that he was heading home a little earlier than usual this day to put a new engine in his car. Somewhat surprised by his comment, I proceeded to ask why he was doing this. "Is this a task that you like or enjoy doing? Do you *want* to put a new engine in your car?" Jerry proceeded to answer my question with "Well, I can't say I will enjoy putting in the engine, but I know I can do it over a few days and it will probably save me about $750."

I drove away with the conversation racing in my mind. So there was Jerry, a very capable and talented leader—so much so that he could put a new *engine* in his car—who was neither intimidated by a complex and somewhat risky project nor unwilling to do the hard work it would surely take to complete; and all this to save some money. Jerry had just put in a full day at the office and was now willing to spend the first of several evenings working at home for 750 bucks in savings. Questions were spinning in my head. First, who changes their own engine? What a stud! Next, how do Jerry's wife and daughter feel about all this, him working in the garage for several evenings and away from the family? Are they supportive of these activities? Finally, as a business leader, what can *we* do to tap into the talents, ambitions, and abilities of our truly underutilized employees like Jerry?

Fact was our business had dozens if not hundreds of opportunities for improvement that were worth millions of dollars in total. And I knew that the *only* way those opportunities would come to fruition was through the minds and hands of our leaders and their teams. We needed the very best of Jerry and others, and we needed them desperately! I couldn't afford to underutilize or waste the potential within our employees by simply valuing and compensating them for their time and attendance. Rather, the challenge was to unleash the capacity, innovation, self-initiative, and ambition that were almost oozing out of Jerry and others. Employees were already sending signals that they had more to offer and a desire to do so. The key was to put ladies and gentlemen like Jerry in the right roles where they could develop and implement smart leadership, strategies, and processes. Properly deployed and directed, Jerry and others could enjoy four- and five-figure financial rewards through incentives if they could find ways to produce five- and six-figure results for the company. And I knew they could!

Is Your Best Talent Leaving the Building?

I wondered, was Jerry the only employee who believed he needed to "leave the building" to financially benefit his family or himself? No. Many of our employees were making similar decisions to save or earn money apart from the opportunities we offered. These pursuits included side jobs, investments, or businesses. In a few cases, we had even lost good employees to legitimately better jobs and companies elsewhere. Shame on us! We could and had to do better. In fairness, we were a small company and limited in the compensation, benefits, and other resources that we could offer. But the potential for our business was enormous and, if we could just find a way to capture this potential, we would have significantly more resources at our disposal. Resources generated by increased sales, higher margins, lowered expenses, and the resultant increase in profitability could be invested back into our company and people. What if we could share a portion of those gains or savings with the team members that were in the best position to capitalize on them? The concept was somewhat uncommon, but not revolutionary or even that complicated.

As described in detail in our application to receive the Malcolm Baldrige National Quality Award, http://patapsco.nist.gov/Award_ Recipients/PDF_Files/Stoner_Application_Summary.pdf, we began to identify our biggest opportunities and match them with the individuals and teams who were in the best position to pursue them. These teams and work groups proceeded to research and prioritize steps that would move the opportunities forward. Outcomes and key indicators were identified to measure results and progress. Various forms of sharing were established based on the contribution and performance of the team.

The individual responses to our sharing approach were mixed. Some jumped on board with the program quickly, having seen the success of similar plans in previous jobs. Many were motivated by the team-sharing aspect, wanting to be a contributor and not a detractor to the program for the sake of their teammates. Others were simply motivated by the new challenge to achieve results and attain goals that had previously been undeclared or ambiguous.

A remaining few were skeptical right from the start and continued that way for some time. The concerns and hesitation from this group were somewhat reasonable given that they had never experienced a true sharing program or had experienced one that was designed and implemented poorly. Not all of the original naysayers came around, and a very small number eventually found employment elsewhere. Most of the skeptics did eventually come to see how they had valuable and unique contributions they could make to the team and that their contributions led to results that mattered and were rewarded.

Overcoming skeptics and change. I share my experience and challenges above because I realize that any workplace change—and especially one that involves compensation—comes with some uncertainty, skepticism, and fear. I personally believe that people do not fear *change* nearly as much as they fear the *risk* that often comes with change. This book was written to help you consider, plan, and implement changes to the way you compensate your employees while also helping you anticipate and minimize potential risks.

I'm certainly not the first leader to use incentives and sharing. Read on to learn how other organizations of all types and sizes share their success to get results.

"

I noticed that the dynamic range between what an average person could accomplish and what the best person could accomplish was 50 or 100 to 1. Given that, you're well advised to go after the cream of the cream. A small team of A+ players can run circles around a giant team of B and C players.

"

Steve Jobs - co-founder of Apple

Real-World Examples

Public-Company Incentives

I've always been intrigued by *publicly traded* companies, those who issue ownership via stock on open markets like the New York Stock Exchange (NYSE) or NASDAQ. Currently there are around 2,800 companies listed that trade on the NYSE and about 3,100 that trade on NASDAQ. They include seasoned names like Ford, General Electric, and McDonalds and newer names like Tesla, Facebook, and Shake Shack. These approximately 5,900 companies have a combined valuation over $29 trillion![22,23] Together they employ tens of millions of people who generate tens of billions in profit annually.

Publicly traded companies are bought, sold, and owned by investors both within and outside each company. There is hardly a senior leader in any of these organizations that doesn't own a significant portion of the entity they work for through company stock, stock options, or other investment instruments tied directly to the business. Beyond senior leaders, large percentages of employees also own portions of stock in these companies (their employer) where they enjoy gains or suffer losses. Of course, over time the value of stock or ownership generally corresponds to the success or failure of the enterprise. Do you believe there is a significant correlation between stock ownership by employees and the success of these publicly traded companies? How relevant is it that they have "skin in the game?" It's no surprise that many of the best and brightest talent choose to work for publicly traded companies where ownership through stock or other equity instruments is a primary tool for recruiting, engagement, motivation, reward, and retention.

Many of the most successful *privately held* companies, those *not* traded on any stock exchanges but rather owned privately by one or more individuals, also use stock equity-and-appreciation-like *methods* in similar ways to their publicly traded counterparts. They too realize that sharing the company's gains with some or all employees is critical to their success and prosperity.

While the instruments and methods of sharing may vary, leading private organizations, both large *and* small, find creative ways to get the same recruiting, engagement, motivation, productivity, and retention benefits that are commonplace with their successful public-company counterparts.

Big-Sports Example

"We Are." In the state of Pennsylvania, where I'm from, there is a fall tradition that consumes many Keystone State residents. On autumn Saturdays, the tradition is to stop everything and watch Penn State football. Nittany Lion football is a big deal in Pennsylvania, and during home games it's not uncommon to have 106,000+ cheering fans in the seats at Beaver Stadium and thousands more tailgating in nearby parking lots. It's an event worth experiencing to see a Saturday home game in State College. Happy Valley, as this somewhat secluded and seemingly storybook location is affectionately known to fans, was selected by the university's founders back in 1855 partly because of its geographically centered location in the middle of Pennsylvania. In addition to the fans in attendance, millions more watch PSU football on the Big Ten Network and other TV stations. The common rallying cry among fans is "We Are…Penn State!"

Big business. College football at Penn State and elsewhere is big business with layers of participants and beneficiaries. The business starts with university athletic departments that staff administrators, coaches, trainers, assistants, tutors, facilities operators, cooks, travel agents, marketers, merchandisers, and more. Teams require practice fields, training gyms, cafeterias, kitchens, and of course stadiums that now feature corporate boxes, club seats, restaurants, merchandise shops, food vending, press facilities, locker rooms, and many surrounding acres for tailgating and parking of 25,000+ vehicles. In the local communities around each game-day stadium, weekend hotel rooms are booked for months, restaurants enjoy lines out the door, and a variety of merchants gratefully accommodate the influx of fans. We know who they come to watch. According to NCAA rules, each Division I college football team is generally limited to a roster of 105 players carefully selected from among the nation's very best high-school talent. Recruits are enticed with scholarships— eighty-five full scholarships per D1 team—along with the opportunity to play against the best teams in some of the biggest stadiums and the chance to compete among the leading players in the game. In addition to the sport, we can only imagine the other fun, travel, and adventure that these young athletes are able to enjoy.

Big cleats to fill. It's not easy to field a college football team, let alone one that can win. Enormous might understate the pressure that falls upon the staff that's responsible for recruiting, training, conditioning, motivating, and mentoring a group of mostly nineteen- to twenty-three-year-old football players. Certainly, it takes a very talented coaching staff to be successful with no position more important than the head coach.

James Franklin is currently in his fourth year as the head coach of Penn State football. Prior to this role, he was the head coach at Vanderbilt University where he led the program for three years with a record of 24 wins and 15 losses. So how does a high-stakes, high-profile position like head coach of Penn State Football get filled with the best possible candidate? You may be surprised!

Big bucks. Even more critical than the recruiting effort to sign the top collegiate quarterbacks, running backs, and linebackers are the recruiting efforts to attract, negotiate, and close the very best coaches. It would appear that they are among the most important "state employees." By the numbers, they certainly appear to be the most rewarded. In Pennsylvania, no other state employee is paid more than James Franklin. What that means for Pennsylvania residents is that no one in your state is being compensated more with your tax dollars than a football coach. And the amount that I will share with you next is quite astounding. But, before anyone yells "foul," consider that this head coach may be worth every penny.

The highest paid employee in the state of Pennsylvania. According to reports by Pennlive.com and USA Today, James Franklin earns an annual base salary of $4.2 million.[24] This base salary was supplemented with a retention incentive of $300,000 if Franklin was still employed on December 31, 2016—which he was, secured by his season's highlight victory against Ohio State and being named Big 10 Coach of the Year in 2016—and an additional $200,000 if the Lions made a bowl game—which they did: the Rose Bowl against USC on January 2, 2017.[25] No additional incentive for a bowl *win* was noted;

however, it may have existed but would not have paid off in 2017. (Penn State lost to the Trojans by a forty-six-yard field goal in the last seconds with the final score 52–49.)

Big benefits. Do universities like Penn State hire expensive coaching talent foolishly? The numbers prove otherwise. Division I college football brings in billions in annual revenue to participating schools.[26] Penn State football alone reportedly generated revenues over expenses of $36,158,596 for the fiscal year, which ended in mid-2016.[27] Part of this comes from reported media and other per-school annual payments to Big 10 schools of $32,400,000, a number which could potentially double by 2018 thanks in part to new deals with Fox and Disney. After supporting other sports at the university, the PSU athletic department still declared a net profit of over $3 million.[28,29] For this, Nittany Lion fans and business leaders can additionally declare "We are...profitable!"

Government Incentive Example

Pennsylvania Route 11/15 Rock Slope Safety Project. Government projects are rarely known for their efficiency or speed. But one notable project by the Pennsylvania Department of Transportation was the exception in 2016.[30]

In the center of Pennsylvania, a few miles northwest of Harrisburg, a busy stretch of US Route 11/15 runs parallel with the Susquehanna River. One particular one-mile stretch of this roadway near Marysville is pinched tightly between the three-quarter-mile-wide river and a mountain of rock that extends upward 250 feet. Slopes were originally cut into the rock in the 1930s to accommodate the roadway, but time, weathering, freeze-thaw cycles, and vegetation had loosened the rock creating falling-rock safety hazards. Boulders nearly the size of a small car had been known to fall from the slope and onto the road!

PennDOT, the authority responsible for maintaining the roadway, faced several dilemmas. First, the urgency to address worsening safety issues with the road and prevent significant injury or death to roadway travelers. Second, closure of the heavily traveled roadway to make repairs was complicated. With a large mountain on one side and a wide river on the other, the only viable detour route along US Route 22/322 would span twenty-seven miles and take upward of an hour to traverse. Finally, most repairs would need to be performed by heavy equipment during a relatively few summer months. Community pressure to complete the project in a timely manner for economic and community activities was considerable.

A big incentive. PennDOT put out bids for the project months in advance of the spring/summer 2016 project date. The winning contractor was given notice to proceed with the estimated $19,000,000 project in February. The state agency prepared the neighboring communities, commuters, and traveling public that the project would take an estimated ninety days, from May 1 to July 30, during which the roadway would be impassable. The contractor was scheduled to work a minimum of six days a week, fifteen hours per day with several crews to perform multiple tasks. But here's where it got even more interesting:

PennDOT offered incentives to the contractor of up to $50,000 per day and a disincentive of up to $160,000 per day to encourage the contractor to complete the road closure work before ninety days.

Can you imagine what happened? The contractor, J. D. Eckman Inc. was obviously eager and especially motivated to maximize the team's incentive. They reportedly got organized very quickly and set out with an ambitious but clear plan. Up to several dozen workers were scheduled in shifts, around the clock. Being creative, the contractor brought in specialists from Oregon who used heavy-lift helicopters to quickly and efficiently hoist screening mesh up and onto the face of the rock slope.

The result? Through planning, scheduling, innovation *and incentives*, US Route 11/15 was opened to traffic on June 24, *more than a month ahead of schedule.* PennDOT reportedly shared an additional $2,000,000 with J. D. Eckman as negotiated up front for a successful win-win outcome for everyone.

What resources are at your disposal? You may not have access to helicopters and million-dollar incentives, but what resources *are* at your disposal, and how might you *justify innovative incentives* and sharing to achieve significant results?

Some Firsthand Experience and Examples

Service-company example. In recent work with clients, my belief in incentives and sharing continues to be reinforced. With one service-company client, an IncentShare program was implemented to help boost morale, lift productivity, and offset a "culture of overtime" that was being abused by some employees. A simple formula was created where a portion of the results produced by the team was shared monthly. The plan took a few months to take hold and required repeated explanation of the plan intent and how the team of service technicians could significantly influence their results. Company leaders increased communication about the plan benefits and looked for ways to guide and assist the team. One approach was to create a simple one-page outline to guide the outcomes that the service techs could influence. Another was to hold weekly "huddles" where results were presented and analyzed. Within a few months, team behaviors began to change. Communication increased, teamwork improved, and profitability per technician started to rise. Soon the team began to reap the benefits of the gains they were achieving, which resulted in hundreds of additional dollars each month for each tech. In a little over a year's time, company profitability doubled!

Manufacturing-company leadership team example. At another manufactured-products client, the senior leadership team had significant responsibilities but none of which truly emphasized *profitability*. The leaders were subsequently educated about all that was necessary for the business to achieve an annual profit and their unique contribution. Each leader identified several key measures and improvement goals. With a new shared responsibility for profitability and a sharing plan that would reward each leader, the team worked together to prioritize improvements and coordinate changes. Within a few months, after implementing several key changes, company profitability began to rise rapidly. The team's effort continued, eventually transitioning the business from breakeven to a near double-digit percent net profit!

Sales team example. A third client distributes and services capital equipment that typically sells from $10,000 up to $100,000 per transaction. They have built a high-performing sales team that is motivated by the company's culture and incentives to provide world-class care for their clients. Members of the sales team can earn six-figure incomes that are linked directly to the financial and margin performance of their departments. Because most transactions are from repeat customers, the team members strive for and have learned to achieve win-win-win outcomes for their clients, the company, and themselves. Tendencies to oversell or undersell (charge too much, or too little) are kept in balance by the need to "sell today" while also providing genuine value and ensuring client satisfaction so they can also "sell tomorrow." Not surprising, the client's results rank among the top 10% of its peer group nationally!

Administrative work group example. At a fourth client, an administrative staff processed critical data entry and client interactions. Paperwork and information flow was taking weeks to complete with little effort or motivation to improve performance by developing better systems and processes. These back-office roles were critical but were somewhat undersupported and underappreciated by front-end sales and executive leadership members. One solution was to provide additional training, technical support, and implement a sharing plan where cost-saving improvements from more efficient throughput would be shared with the team as a "pie" that would be divided among the team. It took some time for the team to understand how improvements in throughput would benefit the team or themselves directly. With support, coaching, and communication, the back-office team gradually began to improve and see the benefits. Key indicators were identified for the group and linked to financial rewards that were distributed quarterly. Not only did the business results in their work group improve—faster throughput of information with automation or the elimination of unnecessary steps—but morale within the team and appreciation external to the work group also increased. Improvement-sharing payouts increased which reinforced improvement behaviors and rewarded the work group's effort and willingness to change. What began as a group of six people was eventually reduced to four through job reassignment and all with *faster* overall information processing and throughput in the work group.

Recruiting Peak Performers with Incentives

One of the highlights of my career has been the opportunity to work with peak performers. To clarify, these are individuals I would categorize in the top 5% relative to their peers, based on performance. Among these people, some were exceptionally gifted, others were notably experienced, and many simply worked very hard to get amazing results. What's always been interesting to me is that virtually *everyone* I've worked with exhibited peak performance *in at least one aspect* of his or her personality, role, or job. I have come to believe that everyone is uniquely gifted, and the sooner you can discover and make the most of your gifts, the faster you will achieve great things. Special is the person who has been able to *evolve one or combine several* of his or her gifts, experience, or effort to achieve exceptional organization outcomes, most notably those that positively impact others.

Great business leaders pursue peak performers. My appreciation for this started early in my career when I was hired as a manufacturing engineer at General Electric. My boss—a few levels up!—was a fast-rising performer named Jack Welch. As the youngest chairman and CEO ever selected by GE, Jack went on to lead GE for twenty years and confirm his peak-performer status by growing the value of the company's stock by 4,000%. Jack Welch became well known for his somewhat controversial approach to take the top 20% of his leaders and fast-track them forward. Alternately, he would send the bottom 10% to find opportunities elsewhere. Welch rationalized that it was actually better to be honest with lower-performing leaders and free them to pursue roles and employers that better matched their abilities and interests. Many who left did indeed go on and find great success at careers that more closely fit their talents.

Various experts and authors have studied and written about peak performers. Bradford Smart wrote a book that highlighted GE's hiring practices under Welch called *Topgrading: How Leading Companies Win by Hiring, Coaching, and Keeping the Best People*. *Topgrading* emphasizes the importance of finding the ideal candidate for each position and building a talented team of "A Players." In *Good to Great*, author Jim Collins famously described the importance of getting "the right people in the right seats on the bus." Collins adds that the right people are not only self-motivated, they also more easily adapt to a fast-changing world.

Consider Google. A fascinating, recently published book called *Work Rules* provides insights about the hiring and workplace practices at Google, now officially known as Alphabet.[31] The book was written by Laszlo Bock, the senior vice president of People Operations at Google who, perhaps not ironically, was recruited out of General Electric. Laszlo joined Google in 2006, two years after its public stock offering, and helped lead the growth of Google's talent pool from 6,000 to almost 60,000 employees. Their mission: "to organize the world's information and make it universally accessible and useful." As you can imagine, Google is no ordinary employer, having been selected seven times by *Fortune* as the "Best Company to Work For" in America. According to Laszlo and per LinkedIn, Google is the most sought after and selective place to work. It receives more than 2,000,000 employment applications annually but hires only several thousand. This makes Google twenty-five times more selective than Yale, Princeton, or Harvard!

Why be so selective? Laszlo's experience is that employee performance does not follow a "bell curve" distribution. Rather, employees perform according to a "power law" curve where a special few employees contribute significantly more than others and in some cases as much as ten to one hundred times. Bill Gates took this thinking a step further stating "a great writer of software code is worth 10,000 times the price of an average writer." With this belief, a key objective is to "stack your team" with recruiting, hiring, and workplace practices that allow you to identify, attract, and retain the very best talent for each position.

Laszlo claims that talented people are increasingly mobile, connected, and discoverable to willing employers. But have employers done their part to be sufficiently engaging, rewarding, flexible, and culturally satisfying to attract and fulfill this select group? High-level talent will flow to organizations that do purposeful work with high levels of freedom and low levels of bureaucracy and provide commensurate rewards and satisfaction. In high-performance environments, people are motivated and behave like entrepreneurs and owners who are willing to do whatever is needed to make the organization successful.

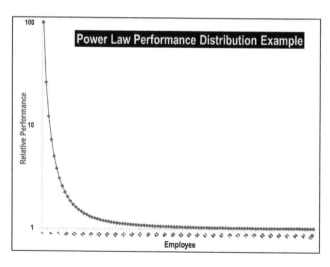

Google cofounder Sergey Brin declared early on that his employees are "everything" and that the company was focused on attracting and leveraging technologists and business people with "exceptional talent." In exchange, Sergey committed to "reward and treat them well." What does this look like? First, Google hires slowly, being mindful that only 10% of its applicants at best would truly be top performers. The company claimed to spend twice as much time and effort as its peers to attract and select new employees. Second, only hire people who are "better than you," which requires a significant degree of both selectivity and humility on the part of the hiring leader or team. Finally, Google rewards performance generously, celebrates it publicly, and grants stock to all employees making them long-term stakeholders in the outcomes of the enterprise.

Compensation at Google. Next to recruiting, compensation issues and how to pay people fairly is reportedly where people managers at Google spend most of their time. In the early days, talented employees were known to take pay cuts, believing in the company and future rewards. Some new hires were given the choice to gain 5,000 stock options in exchange for $5,000 of salary. It apparently was a good deal, since Googlers who accepted the risk eventually returned $5,000,000 for their gamble. Today, Google still believes in paying people "unfairly," partly by making every employee eligible for stock awards based primarily on performance. Sergey states, "We believe strongly in being generous with our greatest contributors." Laszlo confirms, "Your best people are better than you think, and worth more than you pay them."

How do you recruit and reward your peak performers? Do you acknowledge the difference that some individuals or work groups could contribute to your success? When you hire, how often are extraordinary candidates forced into a pay scale or compensation plan that's based solely on an industry average or standard? Rather than offer an oversized salary, how can you use innovative rewards and compensation strategies to more fairly or more generously compensate for results and therefore entice exceptional talent? Are you willing and able to explore compensation options that might require slightly more innovation and planning, or are you restricted to compensation approaches that are simply easy to administer?

If you wanted to recruit and reward for peak performance, how might you create a plan to do this effectively and efficiently? Consider first, what performance results contribute the most value to the organization. Next, identify which individuals or work groups most impact specific contributing results. Formulate simple ways to share a portion of these results or improvements with the primary contributors. Communicate up-front how you appreciate, acknowledge, and reward results in your organization, and watch how peak performance is unleashed among your employees, especially your high potential new recruits.

Are you ready? Each of these stories provides examples of how *others* have used incentives and sharing to improve an organizational result and incrementally benefit individuals or work groups. But how do *you* create sharing plans to enjoy similar benefits? Read on to learn *how* to develop and implement IncentShare plans.

First-rate people hire
first-rate people;
second-rate people hire
third-rate people.

Leo Rosten - American humorist

Part 3:
How to Develop and Implement IncentShare Plans

IncentShare: Step by Step

1. Philosophy
2. Potential
3. Participants
4. Performance
5. People
6. Perceptions
7. Plans
8. Period
9. Portion
10. Payouts
11. Privacy
12. Pitfalls
13. Pullbacks
14. Police
15. Persistence

None of the Fifteen Steps Stands Alone.

As you read through the following pages and fifteen steps to develop and implement IncentShare plans, keep in mind that none of these steps stands alone. Rather, they all work together to help you structure your plans, engage and involve people in the process, implement the plans with work groups or individuals, and evolve as needed to meet changing circumstances and requirements.

If your role is to research, design, approve, implement, troubleshoot, or improve a sharing plan, the following fifteen steps can help guide your thinking and approach.

*Do not neglect to do good
and to share what you have,
for such sacrifices are
pleasing to God.*

Hebrews 13:16 ESV

Fifteen Steps to IncentShare

1. Philosophy—Does the concept of "success sharing" make sense for your organization and team?
2. Potential—What are your opportunities, your goals, and the value of these to the organization?
3. Participants—How is your workforce organized by work group, and who are the participants in each?
4. Performance—What outcomes or results are you seeking from each work group, and how will you measure them?
5. People—Are you prepared to make and communicate sharing decisions that will significantly affect individuals?
6. Perceptions—Good or bad, what experience have others had with variable compensation and incentives?
7. Plans—Who, why, when, how, options, amounts, factors, proportions, scenarios, transparency, and more!
8. Period—What frequency is best to assess results, calculate sharing portions, and distribute to team?
9. Portion—What is the optimum amount to share—enough to be relevant without putting the organization at risk?
10. Payouts—How to manage processing, expectations, variation, good times, bad times?
11. Privacy—What is the appropriate level of privacy and discretion when dealing with individual compensation?
12. Pitfalls—How to optimize results while minimizing risks and surprises, and what about exceptions?
13. Pullbacks—What if an error or misjudgment results in a situation where a plan change or pullback is needed?
14. Police—How to keep plans legal, compliant, within regulatory guidelines, simple, and transparent.
15. Persistence—Are you sufficiently committed to plan, monitor, payout, stay the course, and evolve?

Philosophy

Develop *Philosophical* Support Among Top Leadership.

An initial step in the IncentSharing process is for the leadership to develop and strengthen their philosophical position and rationale for using "sharing as a strategy." Not everyone may see this approach as logical or viable. As leaders, better to put yourselves to the test first to challenge, strengthen, and then communicate your reasons and justification for an incentive or sharing approach. Some may believe that the organization can't afford to share more than is currently being distributed as compensation and benefits. Others may believe that the organization already compensates employees well—if not generously—for their contribution to the team. Still others will fear future unknowns and how incentive commitments might affect the organization.

Overall, many will simply be uneasy about changing the way you have done things in the past. Some of these concerns are legitimate but most can be overcome with proper planning and implementation. A strong philosophical foundation that supports *why* you believe IncentSharing makes sense will equip you to address concerns and strengthen your plans over time.

Potential

Clarify the *Potential* Opportunities Available to Your Organization.

If you have a leadership role in your organization, you are surely aware of opportunities. Clarifying those opportunities is a key responsibility for leaders. Each organization has unique opportunities, but the list below may help you identify both obvious and not-so-obvious improvement areas to consider:

Sales growth
New customers
Better customers
Higher pricing
Bigger orders
Better margins
Lower costs
Higher profitability
Faster payment
Debt reduction
Wealth creation

Facility improvements
Equipment improvements
Preventive maintenance
New products
New services
Faster shipments
Quicker deliveries
Service contracts
Replacement parts
Recurring revenues
Team morale

Effective recruiting	Greater productivity
Training and development	Reduced scrap and waste
Talent retention	Energy savings
Higher engagement	Work-life balance
Better teamwork	Fun and freedom

What other opportunities would you add to the list above? How would you prioritize them? You might consider how quick, easy, or no-cost/low-cost you anticipate they will be to implement. Another approach to consider is the "opportunity value" of the improvement. Look into the future and calculate the financial impact of your improvements over time. How would you value those gains when compounded over one, three, five, or even ten years?

Quantifying opportunities can be difficult, and you will likely need to estimate or consider various future scenarios. This is a critical step however because you will need to compare the value of your opportunities over time to help you prioritize them. Targeting specific and quantified opportunities is essential to help your employees see how IncentSharing can benefit the organization, their work groups, and themselves.

Use "opportunity math" to determine the value of improvement over time. Time is often underappreciated when making improvement decisions. Do you adequately consider the impact of decision-making delays or procrastination in addition to the impact your decisions will have over time? What does your *decision-making process* look like and how long does it take? What is the opportunity cost to defer or delay a decision? Calculate the value of your opportunities over the period of a year and then proportionally by month, week, and day. Motivation will grow when you quantify opportunities and then act decisively on those with the most impact.

Opportunity math is a simple way to calculate the value of your opportunities over time. For example, consider a million-dollar annual opportunity. If your organization has the potential to realize a million dollars of new, untapped, or hidden opportunity in a year's time, that divides down to about $20,000 per week or $4,000 per workday.

Opportunity Math:

$1,000,000 annual opportunity / 50 work-weeks = $20,000 / workweek

$20,000 opportunity / workweek = $4,000 / workday

Do your best to attach a value to your improvement ideas, and be mindful of how that value compounds over time. Like well-invested money, improvement gains can grow in value exponentially.

Participants

Categorize IncentShare *Participants* by Work group.

Rarely does one size fit all when it comes to IncentSharing. Rather, sharing plans are typically best developed for different work groups. This does *not* mean that each work group *must* have a different plan, but each work group should at least be evaluated by the unique contribution it provides. This issue can create some tension. Some believe that "each person makes a unique contribution and therefore should be considered individually." Others believe that organizations succeed or fail as a whole, and everyone should be considered "equally on the team."

In reality, most organizations find a balance somewhere in the middle, and the balance is often influenced by a desire to consider the uniqueness of each *work group* while also striving for a reasonably low number of work group plans for *simplicity*. For example, it often makes sense for a sales work group to have a different sharing plan than a manufacturing work group because of the uniquely different contributions they make. Alternately, it may make sense for a factory maintenance team that services manufacturing equipment to have a very similar or even the *same* sharing plan as the manufacturing team it supports, rationalizing that their roles and proximity are so closely related.

It's Generally Best to Implement IncentShare Plans One Work group at a Time.

Most organizations can benefit by having IncentSharing plans for each of their work groups. However for practical reasons, it's generally advisable to implement IncentSharing plans one work group at a time. The reason for this is partly because of the steps needed to develop an effective plan for each work group, engage work group participants in the process, launch and implement the plan successfully, and monitor and evolve each plan over time. Sequencing work groups one at a time will allow for more attention to detail to help ensure a more successful plan outcome.

This is especially true for the first work group. The timing and pace that other work groups can be added will be dependent on your organization's resources to work through IncentShare steps with each work group. For most organizations, the second, third, and subsequent work group plans roll out easier and faster.

Prioritize in what work group order to develop and implement IncentSharing. As you consider the work-group order, keep these two thoughts in mind: which work groups would most benefit from a plan, and which work groups have the most impact on the organization. Consider the following suggestion that comes from both experience and logic:

Start with your top leaders. I generally suggest you start IncentSharing with your senior leadership team. Consider your senior leaders a "work group" and start with them first. There are a number of ways to select who to include among a senior leadership team, but the list below may help clarify some criteria and reasoning.

Possible Criteria for Selecting Your Senior Leadership Team:

- Owner(s) and/or investor(s)
- Top "C Level" executives (CEO, COO, CFO, etc.)
- Your most "strategic" leaders
- Leaders who have the "most impact" on results
- Leaders considered to be "running the organization"

If you pay peanuts,
you get monkeys.

Chinese Proverb

Performance

Determine What *Performance* is Expected and Best Measures Each Work group.

Because an important outcome of IncentSharing is to share the success of the organization with individuals in work groups, it is essential you decide what indicates success for each work group and how performance results will be measured. For some work groups, determining performance will be obvious. For example, with a sales work group, performance indicators will likely be selected from among sales revenue, sales growth, new customers, repeat customers, customer retention, sales margins, margin growth, net profit, profit growth, etc. These are typically easy-to-quantify and readily available numbers.

For other work groups, determining performance could be more difficult. For example, with a customer-service work group, customer satisfaction would certainly be a critical outcome, but how does it get measured? You might find value in having customers "rate" their satisfaction with your customer-service work group, but how would you implement a process that is thorough, consistent, and gets full participation? In other words, some result measures are much easier and consistent to capture and quantify than others. Certainly, you can get a clear measure of sales revenue, but it is nearly impossible to reliably and consistently measure customer satisfaction. In the case of a customer-service work group, for example, customer retention, sales, gross margin, complaint logs, or net promoter scores (NPS) could be more relevant indicators. If compensation will be linked to results indicators, it's critical that plan participants trust the indicators to be reliable and consistent. Inevitably, some creativity or compromise will be necessary to determine the optimal measure of results and success for some work groups.

Consider this Success Indicator for Your Senior Leaders.

If starting an IncentShare plan with your senior leaders makes sense to you as mentioned earlier, you will need to decide what success indicator(s) would be best to determine sharing. What are the top outcomes or results you desire for your organization? Are there one, two, or three indicators that have a greater impact on your current and future success? Using the Pareto principle, which 20% of your outcomes do you believe has an 80% impact on your viability and prosperity? (See page 172 for more on the Pareto Principle.) Additionally, which of these outcomes can you measure quickly, accurately, and consistently? Here's a suggestion:

With Your Senior-Leader Work Group, Share a Portion of Your Net Profitability.

There are several reasons why sharing a portion of your net profit or EBITDA (Earnings Before payments of Interest, Taxes, Depreciation, and Amortization are deducted) with senior leaders makes sense. First, for many organizations the net profitability or net contribution is at or near the top of their critical outcomes or success indicators. One perspective I've heard is that "profits keep us free," which means that without profit we will ultimately suffer loss of resources, loss of working capital, loss of reinvestment, and ultimately loss of the organization itself. Certainly, profitability is not the only indicator of an organization's success, but it is critical for most. Second, profit is generally a hard and fixed number that viable organizations measure and report consistently with generally accepted accounting practices. It's a business indicator we can access and trust with relatively high confidence. Third, the "challenge of generating a profit" involves many steps and variables that are an appropriate concern for senior leadership in an organization. To make a profit, an organization must proceed successfully through a gauntlet of steps that may include up-front planning, research, development, design, testing, manufacturing, warehousing, marketing, sales, customer service, shipment, delivery, invoicing, servicing, accounting, IT and HR management, and much more. The burden of "making a profit" doesn't typically weigh on the shoulders of *all* employees as much as it does on *some*—those in senior leadership. For them, profitability is a critical responsibility.

Each organization is unique, and profitability isn't the only success indicator that could be shared with senior leaders. If the organization is carrying debt or desires to build asset value or equity, then a measure of debt reduction or wealth creation might be a relevant indicator. If the plan is to sell the business, then senior leaders might participate in a portion of the net or incremental value they create from some designated starting point to the time of sale. Milestone events, like business acquisitions or divestures, getting a key customer, or attaining a sales threshold with a new product or service, could also be used to trigger a predetermined fixed or proportional payout.

People

Because *People* are Involved, IncentSharing Decisions Can Be Very Emotional.

Any action that affects a person's compensation will be emotionally charged. It's important for you to recognize this and take prudent steps to address and comfort people's concerns. It would be naïve to believe that most people will assume your best intentions. Rather, it might be prudent to expect some skepticism and fear among participants and work to eliminate or minimize as many of their concerns as possible ahead of time. This is why it's so important to challenge your intentions early and up-front philosophically so you will be better positioned to anticipate concerns, address issues, and increase alignment among your top leaders, owners, and investors in the IncentShare planning stage. Even with the best-developed plans, some will be skeptical, hesitant, and possibly even resistant. Be prepared by anticipating these reactions and how you will respond.

Below is a sample scripted dialog that may help guide your thinking and how to communicate your desire and intentions for IncentSharing with your team. Ideally, this might be expressed first to your top leaders or a starting group as an introductory overview, ahead of any presentation that includes a detailed plan:

"Thanks for being here. As you know, we've been committed to this business and making it better for our clients, owners, investors, and all of you since we started! We believe that our best days are ahead, and we have some big opportunities.

For some time now, we've wanted to find a good way to 'share our success' with each of you as we make improvements, get better, and grow. We believe 'the more we share, the more we will succeed, and in turn the more we succeed, the more we will be able to share.' The concept is really quite simple, but there are some details we need to clarify to make it all work. We've been researching this and found a resource, IncentShare, that can help us accomplish it!

The idea is if we can find ways to make this organization better, more efficient, more profitable, and grow in healthy ways, then we want to share our improved results and success with the work groups and employees that can get us there. How this would be structured for each work group needs to be worked out in the near future. We will likely proceed somewhat slowly and cautiously, one work group at a time, but our desire is to one day have everyone in this organization sharing proportionally somehow in our success.

At this point we mostly want to make you aware of our intentions, and bring you up-to-date on some work we have done. We'll be selecting one or several work groups to start with and connecting with the work-group leaders to discuss how this could work. As with any plan, there will certainly be some learning and evolving as we go. We would appreciate your patience, understanding, and support as we work together on this. Our intent is for the plan to be significantly positive for our organization and significantly beneficial for all of you!"

Perceptions

Ask Questions to Uncover Participant's Concerns and *Perceptions*.

The best way to minimize concerns and maximize support for an IncentShare program may simply be to ask questions and get feedback. Some people have had no exposure and others extensive experience with incentives and variable compensation programs. Good or bad, what are your employees' perceptions? Past experience or preconceived notions about incentives could be a significant hurdle for you. Or it could be a tailwind! It's important to get input from participants, especially your leaders, to address their questions, concerns, and exposure to incentives, variable compensation, and sharing. It's better to hear and respond to pros and cons up-front than to let concerns go unspoken and unaddressed. Here are some questions to ask of your team:

- What *opportunities* do you see ahead for our organization and what is our potential?
- What is *holding us back* and what would bridge the gap between current results and our potential?

- How big a factor is *motivation and engagement* among our workforce?

- What *results might we achieve* if we found a way to "share our success" with more of our team?

- What *experience* have you had—good or bad—with incentives or variable compensation plans?

- What *concerns or questions* do you have regarding sharing via incentives?

Plans

Creating the Sharing *Plan* or Formula

Virtually every sharing plan results in a formula or equation from which a portion of sharing is calculated for each participant. The best formulas are designed to both motivate individual performance to accomplish the organization's objectives *and* be simple and transparent enough to be clearly understood. There are so many variables and ways to create these formulas that it would be impossible to show them all here. It *is* possible however, to provide an *example* formula for one work group and to illustrate a few formula variants. For the sake of this exercise, we will use the senior-leader work group example mentioned earlier. We will illustrate some formula options to share a portion of the organization's profitability with them as previously suggested. To get started, we will need some information—specifically how many senior leaders will be included in the plan and what the organization's profitability was for a given period:

Organization's Profitability for a Period   **$$$**
Number of Senior-Leader Participants   **#**

As we continue to devise a plan for sharing, it would be prudent to understand the history of the organization and how these values have changed in the past one, three, five, or more years. The relevant question is "Where have we been or come from?" Additionally, it would be wise to look ahead and anticipate what these numbers might be in our future. How well can we predict these values looking forward? "Where are we headed?"

Period

Over What *Period* of Time
Should Results Be Monitored and Shared?

As you look back at your historical results and ahead at your future expectations, you will need to select a period of time over which you measure these results—yearly, quarterly, monthly, weekly, etc. For many organizations, compiling these numbers somewhere between monthly and yearly is most relevant. Many businesses use quarterly, or every three months. A great way to show all of this is with a matrix or by using a spreadsheet like Chart 1.

Sophisticated—and moderately expensive—data processing options exist, but consider first how readily available and inexpensive spreadsheet software like Microsoft Excel can make this process simple and give you the following capability and flexibility. Keep in mind these features and benefits of Excel:

- Data elements can be easily *added or removed as rows.*
- Data periods can be easily *added or removed as columns.*
- Results can be *manually entered* and edited in data fields easily.
- Results can be *automatically entered* in data fields with relatively simple programming.
- Data fields can be *formatted for improved visual presentation* and data protection.
- Formulas and calculations can be *quickly embedded* as rows or columns for *better data analysis.*
- The spreadsheet can be formatted, color coded, and designed for *ease of use and visibility.*
- *Charts and other visual representations* can be easily extracted from the data.
- Columns and rows can be *hidden for selective data presentation.*
- *All or part* of the spreadsheet can be *shown, printed, or shared* with others.

Chart 1: Results-Over-Time Matrix Example:

Period (years)	Past	Past	Past	Past	Past	Current	Future	Future	Future	Future	Future
Net Profitability ($,000)	50	60	70	80	90	100	110	120	130	140	150
Senior Leaders (#)	3	3	3	4	4	5	5	6	6	7	8

Results-Over-Time Worksheet:

Period (years)	Past	Past	Past	Past	Past	Current	Future	Future	Future	Future	Future
Net Profitability ($,000)											
Senior Leaders (#)											

Period (years)	Past	Past	Past	Past	Past	Current	Future	Future	Future	Future	Future
Net Profitability ($,000)											
Senior Leaders (#)											

Period (years)	Past	Past	Past	Past	Past	Current	Future	Future	Future	Future	Future
Net Profitability ($,000)											
Senior Leaders (#)											

*Motivation is the art
of getting people to do
what you want them to do
because they want to do it.*

Dwight D. Eisenhower - United States President

Portion

What *Portion* to Share with Work Groups and Individuals is a More Difficult IncentShare Decision.

One of the more difficult decisions when creating an IncentShare plan is how to portion the sharing. What amount of sharing should be distributed based on what success result or value? This again is a decision with many options and variables that is impossible to solve with a single answer. The following are some guidelines that may be helpful as you determine the best decision for your organization:

Sharing Portions Should Have the Following Features:

- Be relevant to current results but also anticipate future improvements and gains; how much better can you—and will you—be in the future? Sharing portions must anticipate these scenarios.

- Be adequate enough to generate genuine motivation but not so much to put the organization's finances at risk or leave inadequate resources for improvements and reinvestment; in general, a significant portion of the organization's financial gains must be retained by the organization, and a proportionally smaller amount should be considered for distribution. Ratios between 1:5 and 1:20 are reasonable.

- It should amount to at least 15% of a person's total compensation within a reasonable amount of time and performance improvement. Less than 15% could be perceived as too insignificant to motivate needed changes in attitude and behavior. I've seen plans that function well result in sharing portions that exceed 50% of an individual's total compensation!

When in doubt regarding sharing portions, start small and look for opportunities to increase amounts of sharing over time as results improve and participants get more familiar with the program. It is *much* easier to increase sharing in the future than to start *too big* and feel pressured to reduce sharing formulas or pullback sharing portions.

Warning

To be clear, it is *strongly* recommended that you take every measure to *not* make reductions or pullbacks in sharing *formulas* or equations once they are put in place. (There are a few exceptions to this, especially as plans evolve over time, which we will cover later.) This does not mean that sharing *payouts* shouldn't decline or be reduced proportional to organization's *results* or performance. After all, this is the intention of these plans, that they rise or fall based on the workgroup results that the participants influence! Payouts can and will vary from period to period based on results, but avoid having payouts decline because you "changed the rules by altering the formula" after it has been established. The best way to change sharing formulas if necessary is over a period of time with adequate reasoning, communication, fairness, and in some cases "transition accommodations."

It should go without saying that any *manipulation* of numbers, calculations, or results that are designed to reduce or cheat participants will ultimately be uncovered resulting in drastic consequences to morale, teamwork, trust, performance, and the viability of the organization itself. *Don't even think about* cheating the plan or participants. It's not worth it morally, ethically, or legally, and severe consequences could result.

Three Sharing Examples for Senior Leaders

Let's return to our senior-leader example and IncentSharing based on profitability. We'll use the sample numbers from Chart 1 to establish some sharing values and proportions. Consider the following *three ways*—from among several dozen possible approaches—to share profitability with senior leaders:

A. Share an "equal percent of profit" with each leader.
B. Share a "piece of the profit pie" with each leader.
C. Share a "stacked, two-part ratio" of profit with each leader.

(See also Chart 1 as a reference for the examples that follow.)

A. Share an "Equal Percent of Profit" with Each Leader.

This is the simplest approach that is accomplished by selecting a percent (%) of net profit ($)—EBITDA or similar determination of organization's profitability, *not* sales revenue or gross profit—to share with (N) senior leaders. Let's assume we decide to share 2% of the "Current Year" net profit from Chart 1 with *each* of the five leaders in our example:

IncentShare portion for each Senior Leader
= X% of Net Profit for N Leaders
= (X% x Net Profit) x N
= (2% x $100,000) x 5
= $2,000 each x 5
= $10,000 total

In the "equal percent of profit" example above, if the number of senior leaders increases or decreases, there would be an equal percent of profit distributed for each leader, or $2,000 each.

B. Share a "Piece of the Profit Pie" with Each Leader.

This is another simple approach that varies just slightly from the example above. In this plan, a fixed portion of profits, or a "piece of the pie," is divided among the senior leaders. In the example below, we'll assume the pieces are shared equally; however, it is certainly possible to share unequal pieces of the pie. Determine a percentage of net profit to share and then divide that portion among whatever number of senior leaders you choose to include: (%) of net profit ($) divided among (N) number of senior leaders. Let's assume that we decide to *equally distribute* 12% of the "Current Year" net profit from Chart 1 among all the leaders in our example:

IncentShare portion of net profit,
shared equally among all Senior Leaders
= X% of Net Profit "pie" shared among N people
= (X% x Net Profit) / N
= (12%) x ($100,000) / 5
= $12,000 total / 5
= $2,400 each

In the "piece of the profit pie" example above, if the number of senior leaders increases or decreases, the fixed pie amount would be simply divided among more or fewer participants. This approach is somewhat more complicated but allows for a more controlled and predictable "profit distribution" from the business. If senior leaders can grow the pie without adding additional leaders, they benefit from "the same portion of a bigger pie." As senior leaders are added, the leaders will have to consider if "sharing an additional pie piece" will be more than offset by the incremental contribution of the added leader.

C. Share a "Stacked, Two-Part Ratio of Profit" with Each Leader.

In this third example, the IncentSharing formula gets slightly more complex but can be worthwhile for the purpose it serves and the incremental motivation it can produce. The idea is to share one portion of profit with senior leaders up to a threshold, and share an even *greater* portion of profit with leaders *above* the threshold. The general thinking is that incremental effort, results, and profitability are disproportionately beneficial to the organization, so share the disproportionate benefit with the participants. (After fixed costs and expenses are covered, incremental revenue can result in a much higher contribution to "bottom-line" profit. In addition, a stacked, two-part sharing plan can reduce the tendency to "get comfortable and pull back" at a higher level of results but rather motivate work groups and individuals to take increasing advantage of incremental results and sharing benefits.) Here's one simple senior leadership formula to accomplish this. Determine a percentage of net profit that will be shared up to a threshold level—based on a set dollar ($) threshold or based on a set percent-profit-to-sales (%)—and an additional or incremental percentage of net profit that will be shared above that threshold.

Here's how it can look as a formula, and let's assume that 1 percent of net profit will be shared with each senior leader up to $60,000 of net profit and 3% of net profit will be shared above the threshold of $60,000. Assuming a net profit of $100,000 and five senior leaders, here's how this would work:

$$\text{IncentShare portion of net profit,}$$
$$\text{to be shared (at two levels) equally}$$
$$\text{among all Senior Leaders}$$
$$= X\% \text{ of Net Profit up to Threshold \$,}$$
$$\text{and } Y\% \text{ of NP shared above Threshold \$}$$
$$= ((X\% \times \text{Net Profit} < T) + (Y\% \times \text{Net Profit} > T)) \times N$$
$$= ((1\% \times \$60{,}000) + (3\% \times \$40{,}000)) \times 5$$
$$= ((\$600) + (\$1{,}200)) \times 5$$
$$= \$1{,}800 \text{ each} \times 5$$
$$= \$9{,}000 \text{ total}$$

In the "stacked, two-part ratio of profit" example above, each incremental dollar of profit added above the threshold will pay three times more than profits below the threshold! In a sense, "the last profits made are worth much more than the first, encouraging participants to continue to look for improvement opportunities and be careful to not let focus, effort, or results diminish as the performance period progresses."

Create the Plan and Formula that Best Meets Your Objectives.

Remember that simple rounded numbers were used in the examples above for illustration purposes. Values, percentages, ratios, factors, and equations can be altered or refined as needed to create

IncentShare plans and formulas to best serve your objectives. Selecting a starting point may be your biggest hurdle, and refinements over time are inevitable. Starting small, simple, and conservatively is one way to accomplish this.

You Have Unlimited Flexibility and Options.

You can now imagine how much flexibility and how many options you have available to you when IncentSharing. As you can see, the value of having both past (historical) and future (trajectory) result indicators is critical to anticipate and plan for the different scenarios that you may encounter when IncentSharing. If at this point your concerns—or confusion!—have increased, realize that you can start any plan simply and conservatively and enhance or expand it as you get more comfortable and confident with the gains and benefits you can realize. Also know that we have resources at www.IncentShare. com to help you!

Payouts

Select a *Payout* Period that Optimizes Participant Engagement and the Organization's Infrastructure.

Many organizations traditionally compile and compare their results over the time span of a year. Some use a traditional December 31 year-end calendar, and others use a fiscal calendar with a start and end date that typically corresponds with a month or calendar quarter end. One approach might be to IncentShare *once a year* based on a full year of performance. While this might make sense for some organizations, it's *far too infrequent* to accomplish most sharing objectives.

A far better payout period to consider is *monthly or quarterly*, and here's why: each sharing period, and specifically the "sharing event or payout," is a key opportunity to reinforce the overall objectives and goals of the plan. Additionally, each payout provides feedback to the team regarding work group and individual results and performance during the most recent period. Having only one payout event per year usually puts too much time and distance between behaviors, results, and the corresponding rewards, reinforcement, and paycheck. Too much opportunity gets lost if payout periods are too infrequent.

Payout periods that are too frequent—like weekly—can cause excessive burden on the organization to monitor, calculate, and distribute. Plus, result values and sharing amounts are likely to vary widely and be potentially confusing to participants if paid too frequently. If distributed at short intervals, incentives will pay out in smaller amounts, which can dilute their perceived value. Also, it's wise to be mindful of your payroll resources and not overburden them with payouts that are distributed too frequently.

Many find payout periods that range from every month (or four weeks) on up to every quarter (or three months) to be ideal. This frequency of payout affords regular "success-sharing" reinforcement while the memory of decisions, effort, actions, and results are still fresh in the minds of the participants. The frequency you choose for each work group is dependent on your specific operation cycles. For senior leaders and participants in similar roles, a quarterly payout period may be adequate to sustain morale without losing any motivational momentum. For other work groups, more frequent monthly (or four-week) payout periods could provide more optimal sharing and performance reinforcement to the individuals and the team.

To summarize, for an IncentShare plan designed to share profitability with senior leaders, consider the following:

1. Current, historical, and anticipated profitability
2. Current, historical, and anticipated number of senior leaders
3. Portion of profitability that will be shared
4. Portion of shared profitability for each leader—same or different
5. Period of time that will be used to measure profitability
6. Frequency of distribution of sharing portions
7. How to handle variations in period results and values
8. A simple matrix or spreadsheet to log results and calculate payouts

Ideally, IncentShare payouts are distributed to participants in a *separate paycheck* to clearly indicate what portion of their compensation has come from incentive or sharing-based earnings.

They are to do good, to be rich in good works, to be generous and ready to share.

1 Timothy 6:18 ESV

Privacy

Privacy and Discretion

Any activity that involves individual compensation and benefits requires an appropriate degree of privacy and discretion. While there may be benefit in having a work group of employees all participate together in an IncentShare plan, this should not imply that any employee should know the compensation of another. Privacy and discretion are essential. Depending on how you structure your plans, it could be that all participants receive an *equal* portion or ratio of sharing or alternatively an *unequal* amount of sharing for various reasons. However your plans are designed and portioned, maintaining a high level of privacy—as you would with any other compensation decision—is appropriate.

Discretion on the part of employees with regard to compensation and sharing payouts is also important. Given the likelihood that various work groups would have different sharing plans and even different results in any given period, it's recommended that participants use appropriate discretion regarding sharing payouts and compensation. You may want to encourage or remind participants of this to avoid awkward or inappropriate situations.

For example, when distributing IncentShare payouts privately to individuals, one leader I know would communicate along these lines:

"I really appreciate your effort and the work you've done to make this IncentShare payout possible. These are my favorite payments to make, and you deserve every penny. I would ask however, that you use appropriate discretion. Please don't leave here and run down the hall yelling at the top of your lungs with excitement, or show up tomorrow in the parking lot with a new Ferrari!"

Yes, this is a somewhat comical approach to address and encourage discretion, but you get the idea and can hopefully see the importance.

Pitfalls

Avoiding or Addressing Some *Pitfalls.*

Do you perceive negatives or see pitfalls with incentive or sharing plans? Yes, there are some, but virtually all of them can be overcome with proper planning and some oversight. Hopefully you will agree that the potential advantages and benefits far outweigh any real or perceived negatives. We'll highlight a few here just to make you aware and suggest some possible solutions:

Poor planning. If you are considering an IncentShare plan, or have something in place already, be careful to plan adequately to ensure your success. IncentShare planning is not "rocket science," but it does require some up-front preparation and structure to increase your degree of success and minimize risk or unexpected outcomes.

Continuing with an outdated incentive plan. Many have attempted to create and implement some type of incentive plan in the past with mixed results. Perhaps the plan you have in place now was adequate and worked at one time when the organization was at a different place and smaller in size. What has changed since then? How can you assess your existing plan's effectiveness, and how willing are you to change or improve? How would others weigh in on this? How many participants does your current plan include? Who else might benefit by being included in an IncentShare plan?

Financial risk. Some fear the financial implications of an IncentShare plan that results in incremental payroll payouts. This is a legitimate concern that must be addressed with the plan structure and formulas. Well-structured plans can significantly minimize or eliminate financial risk to the organization in many ways—for example, by keeping payouts tied only to performance improvements or results above a threshold. Smart plans can be designed to compensate participants generously when organization results are strong and automatically protect the organization with lower compensation payouts when results decline. Many participants will gladly accept this trade-off, gaining greater control over their compensation, which is now linked to results that they can influence or control.

Poor participant perception. Some individuals will see any attempt at IncentSharing as a direct or indirect risk or threat. Much of this will be dependent on their past experience with other incentive attempts that failed or were poorly planned and implemented at other employers—hopefully not their current! Some just won't like the accountability of compensation tied to results. Smart planning and adequate communication are two ways to address these concerns. Embracing a "spirit of sharing" and reinforcing that spirit with action will eventually win over many skeptics.

Lack of teamwork. If sharing is tied to work-group or team performance and results, then what about work groups that struggle or have a poor track record, especially if there are both strong and weak performers within the team? Well, few organizations have work groups with only peak performers that always get good results and where everyone always works together as a team. Some would say that this is the fundamental challenge of any group that works together. One question to ask is, how much *motive or incentive* do individuals within a work group currently have to cooperate, explore, innovate, experiment, and test new ways to work together as a team. How many feel it's easier to "keep my head down" and avoid even trying to make things better? With shared objectives, and rewards that can vary based on how a team performs, you may be pleasantly surprised how teams find new and better ways to get along—and get results— for everyone's benefit.

Goals set too high, or too low. What is your organization's experience with goal setting? Goals can work for or against good sharing plans. Goals that are set too high, or even perceived to be too high, can work against your plan. Invest time and resources upfront to develop realistic goals *and* ways they can be achieved. Be ready to supply training, time, tools, and other resources to support goal attainment. Be careful with goals that are too ambitious or set too far out in the future, and replace or supplement them with progressive steps and milestones. Celebrate your progress and new methods you develop to achieve objectives.

Be as wary of goals that are too low, easy, or shortsighted. Goals you can hit easily are often unexciting and uninspiring. The best IncentShare plans should inspire effort to achieve attainable but stretch goals that reward participants in exciting and energizing ways.

Limiting Employees. With IncentSharing plans in place, most employees will be motivated to see them pay out for themselves and others. Often you will see an initial surge of interest, input, and effort by individuals and teams. It's important to provide an adequate amount of encouragement, resources, and freedom to release the potential of the participants and let their capabilities blossom. Few things will damage this more than stifling bureaucracy or overbearing micromanagement. Certainly, it's important to keep the work group's new energy directed and somewhat contained. Look to provide general guidelines and boundaries, but not so much that you suppress the enthusiasm, creativity, and excitement of your up-motivated team.

External circumstances. Every organization is impacted by the world around it. Weather, local and worldwide economic factors, changing regulations, new technologies, competitors, and the burdens of everyday life continue to challenge us. No one is immune. Given this reality, when considering IncentSharing do you believe that you will be better off in an organization where more work groups and individuals "share in the organization's success" or in an organization where the participants have "less skin in the game?" Many believe that organizations survive, succeed, and thrive best *regardless of the external circumstances* when employees and other stakeholders are more directly linked to the success of the enterprise.

Inaction. Just to keep everything in perspective, your greatest risk with incentives or sharing may be doing nothing at all! What opportunities are you missing by *not* putting in place a strategy and process to get your employees as engaged as possible and more fully committed to your organization's success? You're moving forward. Don't stop. What's the best next step you can take?

Legal. The last but certainly not least pitfall to consider is that of the legal issues related to workplace practices and compensation.

We at IncentShare are not lawyers or legal experts. Rather, the written, verbal, or other communication we offer is intended to give you some knowledge and consideration so that you can make more wise and prudent decisions on your own, ideally with guidance and support from legal or accounting professionals. This issue is significant enough that we will address it separately again in the "Police" section ahead.

Pullbacks

What If a Plan Changes or a *Pullback* is Warranted?

IncentShare plans are designed to increase team and participant engagement, morale, trust, and success. Anything within or related to a plan that works against these design objectives needs to be addressed promptly and carefully. Occasionally, plans don't work as intended or circumstances arise that were not anticipated or considered. In this case it may be necessary to change or "pull back" parts of an IncentShare plan. One big dilemma in these situations is the risk of reducing participant confidence in the plan or worse, trust in the organization and its leaders. Careful plan structuring and scenario planning up-front is the best way to avoid or minimize pullbacks. Patience and avoiding the temptation to react too quickly to circumstances that could prompt plan changes is prudent. Occasionally, erring on the side of generosity with plan participants when changes or pullbacks might otherwise be warranted could be the wisest long-term decision.

It *is possible* that circumstances might prompt you to change or pull back a plan. Some of those circumstances could include significant external events such as a catastrophic economic, weather, political, or military event. A more likely circumstance is a significant internal, marketplace, accounting, or employee event that has substantial impact on your organization. Sometimes an internal accounting error, sharing calculation mistake, or communication misunderstanding results in a situation that warrants resolution with fairness.

Below is a partial list of ways to prepare for or respond to potential change or pullback situations, specifically to maintain trust and integrity in your sharing plan and philosophy:

- Communicate to participants up-front that plans will evolve and may occasionally change.
- Communicate that plan errors are a possibility and will be handled as fairly as possible.
- If discrepancies arise, first reconfirm all data, formulas, and correspondence. Double check to ensure accuracy.
- Maintain accurate financial records and all participant correspondence regarding plans and agreements.
- Ensure accurate data capture and oversight to minimize discrepancies with any results or key indicators.
- If changes or a pullback is justified, communicate to participants but consider delaying implementation to a time in the future.
- For relatively minor issues or errors, it may be prudent to simply absorb the cost and not pass along to participants.
- Consider offsetting necessary long-term changes with a short-term trade-off of compensation or benefits.
- Communicate how changes or pullbacks are justified and/or how other benefits will result.

Police

Keep It Legal-and the Employment *Police* Happy.

Various laws and government regulations govern employment and compensation practices. No information or recommendations provided by the author, IncentShare, VDP123 LLC, or LSP123 LLC representatives are intended to supersede applicable laws or regulations. Neither the author nor any of its representatives are legal or accounting advisors. It is strongly recommended that you consult with both legal and accounting professionals before implementing or making changes to any compensation plan.

One resource for you to consider is the US Department of Labor and specifically tools and guidance for employers from the Wage and Hour Division. See https://www.dol.gov/whd/foremployers.htm. There you will find information that may be relevant to your workplace circumstances and employees, particularly, but not limited to, regulations which pertain to overtime compensation such as those found at Code of Federal Regulations (CFR) Title 29, Part 778, Overtime Compensation.[32]

Whoa, sorry for all the legalese, but it's important.

Persistence

IncentSharing is a *Persistent* Journey.

Considering, planning, structuring, implementing, monitoring, and evolving a plan to share your organization's success typically starts with just a vision and a few ideas that grow and evolve as you learn, launch, and refine your plans. You are off to a good start. Now it's important to sustain your momentum, identify what's next, and find a way to move forward. It is far better to start a plan in a small, simple, and conservative way and then look for opportunities to improve and expand the plan over time.

Once you have launched a plan, it's important to stay the course and not retreat. IncentSharing is sufficiently engaging, exciting, and emotionally charged that you won't want to do anything to damage or reduce the momentum you've created. Challenges, conflicts, and temptations to make quick or reactive changes will occur. Consider them wisely and patiently as you look for the best ways—and best timing—to evolve and improve your IncentShare plans. Certainly, you will end up at a different place than where you started. With diligence, patience, and persistence you, your organization, and your IncentShare participants will almost certainly find yourselves in a better organization, where many are enjoying the benefits of shared success.

There is no joy in possession without sharing.

Erasmus - Renaissance teacher, theologian

Keep It Simple

What about complexity? Some leaders are hesitant to consider variable compensation plans because they perceive them to be complex. They say, "We like the idea of IncentSharing, but how do we keep it simple?" Relax, and know that the best IncentShare plans are often the simplest! Use this book—and visit IncentShare.com—to help you understand the whys, hows, pros, cons, and ways to simplify variable compensation approaches. A fundamental goal of IncentSharing is to design and implement plans that are sufficient enough to achieve the desired organizational results *and* simple enough to be clearly understood by all participants.

Where variable compensation plans can increase in complexity (and decrease in effectiveness) is when they are structured to accommodate too many objectives or variables. Developing plans that address the core or top-level outcomes without getting bogged down in lesser considerations is essential. Often the simplest plans are the most strategic and effective! The good news is that there are numerous ways to reduce or eliminate complexity with smart planning, a straightforward and conservative start-up approach, and a gradual evolution of plans as organizational needs and circumstances change. Almost any organization can have virtually every employee participate in an

IncentShare plan that works effectively, efficiently, and is sustainable for many years.

The Best IncentShare Plans are Sophisticated Enough to Work and Simple Enough to be Easily Understood.

Don't underestimate the importance of careful up-front planning and a willingness to occasionally evolve plans as circumstances change. Many existing incentive plans don't work as intended because they were hastily structured in the beginning or have remained unchanged for too long, leaving them simply out of date. We can help you avoid these pitfalls.

Personal Story

Simple enough for second graders. My wife, Melissa, is one of the most caring, loving, and smartest people I know. Not surprising that she chose as her profession to be a teacher and specifically a reading specialist. Melissa is an avid reader and quick to share a story, character, or classic line from literature. She has great practical sense and, unlike me at times, amazing intuition when it comes to reading people.

Melissa has taught in several schools, always to elementary- or middle-school children. Kids from kindergarten to eighth grade come to Melissa for help with reading and occasionally math. I've learned some valuable leadership lessons from Melissa the educator and even more from Melissa the learning specialist. Countless students have restored their reading skills, many from a multiyear deficit, within the patient and supportive walls of Melissa's classroom.

Here's the classroom problem. Sometimes children don't behave. Further, children's misbehavior often escalates in a classroom environment. Can you picture it? Well, Melissa has some interesting solutions.

Knowing Melissa, it's no surprise to me that she would have ways to manage classroom behavior. What is surprising, is how simple and related her methods are to IncentShare plans!

In today's classrooms, teachers have limited resources to lead—and if necessary command—a room full of students. Most children behave and perform fine but when a few don't, it's a problem. Many teachers and even administrators like principals and superintendents feel as if they have one arm tied behind their back when it comes to all but the worst classroom actors. The challenge is that even a few distracters can squander precious time, resources, and more from other eager-to-learn students.

Something to Give or Take Away

"You need to have something to give or take away from students," says Melissa. "The ability to offer something or withdraw it—within reason of course—gives significant control back to you as a teacher." I know of two approaches that Melissa has used.

One approach helped Melissa when she started teaching as a substitute teacher or *sub.* "Subbing can be the worst because you haven't had a chance to build rapport with the students, and some see an opportunity to grab attention by causing trouble." After suffering through a few rough days as a sub, Melissa developed a plan to regain control of her classroom. Here's how it worked. When one or more students would misbehave, Melissa would simply write an "R" on the classroom board. She would do this in silence without saying a word to the students for enhanced effect! If misbehavior continued, without a word—but with a stern look, I'm sure—Melissa would continue to write on the board with an "E." With each letter, the students would get increasingly curious and then challenged to discover what was happening. At the next indication of students talking among themselves, goofing around, or otherwise misbehaving, Melissa would proceed with another letter: a "C."

Eventually, as letters were added, the students would almost beg to know what was happening, what the letters on the board meant, and what word was being spelled. Melissa would then explain that for each misbehavior she would add another letter to the word "RECESS." If because of bad behavior she had to spell the whole word, then afternoon recess would be *denied*. Everyone in the class would have to stay inside during their beloved recess time. "No, you can't, that would be terrible!" was the almost guaranteed reaction. (It has been quite a few years for me, but do you remember recess as your favorite class of the day?)

However, along with the bad news comes a good option for the students. If classroom behavior *improves*, at the teacher's discretion, a letter may be erased thus giving the class an opportunity to "earn back" letters for good behavior and secure their afternoon recess!

With this incentivized approach, classroom behavior almost always improved, and Melissa gained student respect for her innovative classroom leadership.

The Classroom Store

Melissa's second approach to encourage good classroom behavior and engagement is a little more involved but very effective. I personally think this one is genius.

A sticky secret. Thankfully, my wife Melissa appears to have very few classroom behavior or engagement issues. I credit this to her amazing teaching and personal connection skills, but she shares the credit with…stickers! Apparently, in an elementary- and even a middle-school setting, stickers can have surprising currency value. Here's how it works:

At the beginning of each school year, Melissa explains to the students that if they come to her class, are willing to learn, and try their best, she will reward them each day with a sticker. She sources from the local dollar store a variety of stickers in all shapes, colors, and themes that the students can select on their own. If the student has a good day—meaning follows the classroom rules and tries his or her best—the student gets a sticker. Melissa issues a folder to each student on which they apply and accumulate their sticker earnings. As the school year progresses, competition among the students enhances the approach because students don't want to get behind their peers in sticker accumulation. Stickers as an incentive? Seems so simple and even trivial to me, but apparently it works for these young students. While most days result in sticker-positive reinforcement, I'm told that tears *do* flow on occasion when the thrill of misbehavior fades and the bitter reality of a lost sticker opportunity sets in.

The store. Melissa's sticker approach gets even better. At the end of each school semester, earned stickers can be redeemed for prizes. Melissa calls it "the store," where students get to spend their earned stickers for very small gifts, also from the dollar store, such as school supplies, books, and of course even bigger stickers. A little effort, a few dollars, and some stickers allow Melissa to have a better class environment, more engaged and productive students, and much better classroom outcomes.

Melissa calls it her sticker strategy, but I see a simple innovative IncentShare approach uniquely designed for the work group, which in this case is young classroom students.

Sam's Ten Simple Rules

During my career, I've enjoyed working with and getting to know many amazing organizations and leaders. A few have influenced and inspired me more than others. Two of those were Walmart and Sam Walton. I never knew the man personally, but I've felt his spirit and have seen his impact on numerous occasions. Walmart was a great client of mine earlier in my career, providing distribution for products that we made in our small, rural Pennsylvania manufacturing company. Through Walmart's stores and distribution, our products could be purchased in virtually every midsized town in America and of course at a very reasonable price.

I've enjoyed numerous trips to Walmart's headquarters in the quaint small town of Bentonville, Arkansas. We would travel there to participate in training and meeting sessions in their understated yet somewhat intimidating purchasing and corporate offices. As you can imagine, the best sales and marketing representatives in the world walk through their doors each year, and I was humbled to be among them.

Worldwide, Walmart sells more than $480,000,000,000 in goods and services through 11,500+ physical locations and e-commerce while employing about 2,300,000 employees. In 2016 Walmart returned over $10,000,000,000 to shareholders through dividends and share repurchases.[33]

Whatever your experience with or beliefs about the company, Walmart's story and Sam Walton's legacy is worth knowing.

Sam Walton's Ten Rules

Sam Walton believed running a successful business boils down to ten simple rules that helped Walmart become the global leader it is today. Walmart continues to apply them to every part of its business.[34] Take special note of Rule # 2.

1. **Commit to your business.** Believe in it more than anybody else. If you love your work, you'll be out there every day trying to do it the best you possibly can, and pretty soon everybody around will catch the passion from you—like a fever.

2. **Share your profits with all your associates, and treat them as partners.** In turn, they will treat you as a partner, and together you will all perform beyond your wildest expectations.

3. **Motivate your partners.** Money and ownership alone aren't enough. Set high goals, encourage competition, and then keep score. Don't become too predictable.

4. **Communicate everything you possibly can to your partners.** The more they know, the more they'll understand. The more they understand, the more they'll care. Once they care, there's no stopping them.

5. **Appreciate everything your associates do for the business.** Nothing else can quite substitute for a few well-chosen, well-timed, sincere words of praise. They're absolutely free—and worth a fortune.

6. **Celebrate your success.** Don't take yourself so seriously. Loosen up, and everybody around you will loosen up. Have fun. Show enthusiasm—always. All of this is more important, and more fun, than you think, and it really fools the competition.

7. **Listen to everyone in your company.** And figure out ways to get them talking. To push responsibility down in your organization and to force good ideas to bubble up within it, you must listen to what your associates are trying to tell you.

8. **Exceed your customers' expectations.** Give them what they want—and a little more. Make good on all your mistakes, and don't make excuses—apologize. Stand behind everything you do.

9. **Control your expenses better than your competition.** This is where you can always find the competitive advantage. You can make a lot of different mistakes and still recover if you run an efficient operation. Or you can be brilliant and still go out of business if you're too inefficient.

10. **Swim upstream.** Go the other way. Ignore the conventional wisdom. If everybody else is doing it one way, there's a good chance you can find your niche by going in exactly the opposite direction.

You can read more about Sam Walton's business rules in his book, *Sam Walton, Made in America: My Story.*

Part 4:
How to Support the
IncentShare Workplace

*Get the right people on
the bus and the wrong people
off the bus.*

Jim Collins - author, *Good to Great*

LSP123

Well done. You've been working diligently to design and implement IncentSharing plans for your work groups. Now, what's next?

It's very likely that your leaders and employees are excited about the opportunity they now have to benefit incrementally from your organization's success. Hopefully you've engaged them in the development of your plans with discussion, feedback, surveys, and how you've introduced and communicated your intention for sharing. They will soon realize that their contributions are now even more relevant to the organization, their teammates, and themselves. One of the most important next steps for you is to lead, guide, and support the team's effort.

Every team needs a coach, and every ship needs a captain. But we know that not all coaches and captains perform equally. Why do some leaders achieve greatness and others fail with fanfare? How dependent is success on the people, the plans, or the processes?

A favorite approach I've used to lead and coach teams where IncentShare plans are in place is based on "LSP123." LSP is an acronym that I'll describe in the next chapter and following pages. I've found no other method to be as simple or effective to support and guide work groups successfully.

LSP Overview

LSP—Leadership, Strategy, and Process—is a foundation upon which you can accomplish almost any worthwhile objective. Organizations, work groups, and individuals that focus first on leadership, second on strategy, and third on their processes will get more done in less time and boost their results. LSP in 1-2-3 order is a simple yet powerful approach to guide your leaders and support your workforce.

1. Leadership
2. Strategy
3. Process

What challenges have you experienced or are you facing now? How has LSP impacted those challenges? Whether at home, work, school, or play, consider how the leader's involvement, strategy deployed, and processes used contributed to the success or failure of the effort. Within teams and work groups, or even among family and friends, LSP is critically important. Use LSP to overcome obstacles and capture your opportunities with less risk and reduced effort.

Can you recall a situation in life where the outcome was very successful? Did it involve extraordinary action by one or more leaders? Did they act with a plan or strategy that was then implemented with a methodical approach or process? Alternately, consider a challenge where the outcome wasn't so successful. How did LSP play a part? Was there weak or nonexistent leadership? Did the effort suffer from little or no up-front thinking, organization, or planning? What role did process—or lack of any—play in the outcome? Tap into the power of LSP to improve your outcomes and avoid pitfalls.

No worthwhile objective is accomplished easily. To prosper, you need a disciplined straightforward approach. Learn to leverage the power of LSP so you can achieve your most important objectives in measurably less time.

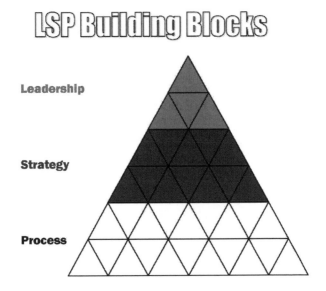

LSP Building Blocks

Leadership

Strategy

Process

Leadership

The word "leader" is one of the most broadly defined terms in the dictionary. The most popular definitions refer to a "person who manages, directs, guides, or commands a group, organization, or country" or "a company or organization that is the most successful or advanced in a particular area." Beyond these definitions, we all have a sense of leadership and its impact on individuals and groups both for good and for bad.

In the context of LSP, I believe that Leadership is the most important component. Many organizations have a relatively few number of "leaders" who have responsibility for the outcomes of the enterprise. Often, the leaders are viewed as a select few or subset of the entire group. I believe that a more accurate—and more powerful—perspective is "leadership at *all* levels," which implies that *everyone on the team has a leadership role and leadership responsibilities.*

However you describe your leaders, consider their relative importance. I believe that leaders have disproportionate impact in the LSP equation. What I mean by this is the role and impact of leaders often exceeds the impact and value of both Strategy and Processes. I often illustrate this with the following graphic:

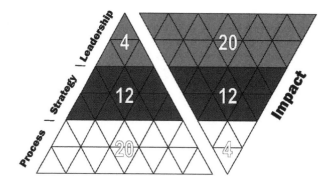

The graphic above shows the relationship between "Leverage" and "Impact" and how the Leadership of a relatively small number of individuals can often have the greatest impact on your results. "As go your leaders...so goes your organization" is the thinking. For good or for bad, leaders have a leveraged impact on your organization that is influenced by many factors, not the least of which are the "hearts and minds" by which they lead.

Leading with "Hearts and Minds"

Leading with "heart" emphasizes the relationships and caring that exist and are developed between leaders and others in the organization. The leaders' relationship *inward* with themselves (self-awareness) and the relationships that leaders foster *outward* with others are both relevant to "heartfelt" leadership. Heartfelt leadership embraces authentic behaviors where individuals are genuinely respected and appreciated, and relationships are highly valued and protected.

Leading with your "mind" acknowledges the wisdom and discernment required of good leaders. In competitive business, marketplace, and other environments, leaders must facilitate and make many decisions. Knowledge, experience, preparation, discipline, and a host of other traits related to making wise choices are critical. One of the most important roles of a leader is to use their *mind* to create great strategy!

Strategy

Strategy can be described as "a plan, method, or series of maneuvers for obtaining a specific goal or result." You may simply think of it as *your plan to get the results you want*. Strategies can vary widely, but don't underestimate their importance. To succeed, leaders must develop great plans or strategies.

To facilitate strategy development with my clients, I've developed a simple planning outline to use as a guide. One of the benefits of the outline is that it can be used at all levels throughout most organizations. What this means is that the outline can be used to guide strategy at the very top of the organization and can also be used as a planning tool at the department, work group, or project level as well. In some cases, the guide can even be used by individuals to define their role and to plan their specific contribution to the larger work group or organization.

The following "Plan to Prosper" diagram illustrates the step-by-step sequence of my strategic planning outline, starting at the top.

LSP123 Plan to Prosper (P2P)

I'll share some details about each step of Plan to Prosper (P2P) in the coming pages, but for now you may just want to get familiar with the stages and progression, starting at the top. Regardless of whether you are using the P2P to help plan a project, department, or entire company or organization, most of the steps apply.

I can't think of a better way to start any team or begin any endeavor than to answer the question "Who are we, and why do we exist?" As you progress around the plan circle, you'll see other relevant steps with equally powerful questions to be answered. Some of these prompt "What are the critical outcomes you wish to achieve," and "how will you go to market with whatever you've created?"

After you have defined your key strategies, one of the next steps will be to create procedures or processes to help you implement your plans. Here's a quick overview of process in the context of LSP, and how you can use processes to more quickly and more easily achieve results.

Process

My favorite way to describe processes is "value-added routines"— *routines* (meaning repetitive) that *add value* (meaning they leave something or someone better off than when the process was started). A simple way to assess or evaluate any process is to look for what, if any, value it created or delivered. How much value is each of *your* processes delivering to others? Which processes are delivering little or no value, and how can they be changed or eliminated?

Bad versus Good Processes

We've all experienced both good and bad processes. For example, think of the last time you visited a restaurant and the processes you enjoyed or endured. Did you have a good experience, bad experience, or a mix of both? Why?

Restaurant experiences give us great *process examples* for a number of reasons. First, we all enjoy good food and friendly service, which makes restaurant dining a very engaging and emotionally heightened event. Second, we've all eaten at restaurants and know the general steps and sequence. Third, we've each dined enough to adequately gauge our experiences from "amazing" to "terrible." Finally, we can all relate to at least a few specific personal restaurant experiences and have some stories to share.

Great dining, as with other great processes, delivers value in the form of products and services that *exceed* your basic expectations. With dining this might mean an experience that does more than just "satisfy your hunger without messing up your order." To exceed your expectations, a chef and server could deliver unexpected extras like amazing flavor, a carefully crafted presentation, and delivery in a prompt, friendly, and gracious way.

LSP123 Overview Illustration:

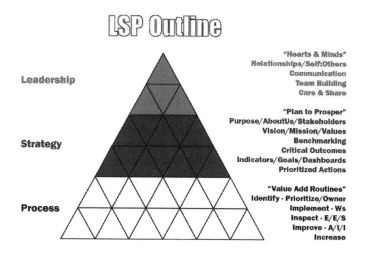

The most dangerous leadership myth is that leaders are born; that there is a genetic factor to leadership. That's nonsense. In fact, the opposite is true. Leaders are made rather than born.

Warren Bennis - leadership scholar

How Do *You* Lead?

Expand Your Leadership Perspective and Potential.

How do you describe leadership? It's not an easy question, but if you're reading this, it's almost certain you're in a position where you really *should* have an answer. There are several ways you might respond. You could choose to define leadership by its dictionary description, which would include something like "*a person* who manages, directs, guides, or commands a group, organization, or country" or "*a company or organization* that is the most successful or advanced in a particular area." Alternatively, you could identify one or several benchmark leaders and proceed to talk about them or their actions as *examples* of leadership. Additionally, you could select some leadership *qualities or values* that best exemplify what leadership means to you. Whatever your response, it's critical to *identify with* a definition of leadership to guide you and those on your team who may look eagerly to you for direction and support.

As a business and volunteer leader for over 25 years, I've wrestled with the definition of leadership many times. Honestly, my personal understanding of leadership has evolved considerably—and thankfully—as I've had repeated opportunities to follow, lead, succeed, fail, win, and lose. The way I define leadership now is far different than how I defined it when I was a much younger, inexperienced, and all-too-often naïve leader. Today, my favorite way to think about leadership is through the simple phrase "It's about hearts and minds."

Simplifying Leadership to Hearts and Minds

I've always enjoyed the mental challenge of trying to simplify a complex concept—like leadership! It's an imperfect exercise, but potentially very valuable if you can find ways to organize complexity into smaller and more basic parts. Simplification can help leaders and their teams enjoy a sharper focus for amplified impact. The 80/20 rule, or Pareto principle, is among my favorite simplification tools. Pareto was a simplifier.

Vilfredo Federico Damaso Pareto (1848–1923) was an Italian engineer, sociologist, economist, political scientist, and philosopher who gave us the 80/20 rule, or Pareto principle. The 80/20 rule, a gift to leaders, states that a relatively small 20% portion of most activities, customers, ideas, approaches, communication, etc. generally results in a disproportionately larger 80% portion of the results, sales, impact, benefits, understanding, etc. The 80/20 rule applies throughout leadership and especially when simplifying. Keeping it simple allows you to clarify what "matters most."[35]

For sure, hearts and minds is a simplified definition of leadership. But don't overlook the power in these words. Let's take a closer look at each.

Leading with Mind

Leading with your mind is the traditional way that many look at leadership. Everyone can relate to a smart or disciplined person or process that helps someone navigate from here to there. *Mind leadership* often includes planning, preparation, implementation, and achievement of a goal or strategy. Many are familiar with mind leadership and some of its traditional components:

- Wisdom and Discernment
- Attitude and Discipline
- Planning and Strategy
- Prioritization and Focus
- Time Management
- Team-building

Leaders can go far with strong mind attributes like those above. But will these qualities alone provide leaders with the resources needed to succeed at their highest potential? I suggest not. There is another aspect of leadership, a resource that all leaders can develop and utilize, and that is leadership with heart.

Leading with Heart

There's a very good chance that you have experienced or delivered leadership with heart. It probably felt different, and you liked it! *Heartfelt leadership* emphasizes human relationships and connection, and typically involves a combination of the following three characteristics:

- Self-awareness
- Others focus
- Communication

Self-awareness. Pastor Bill Hybels says it best: "You are the most difficult person you will ever lead." Are you willing to accept this statement? The more we know, understand, and accept about ourselves, the better we will be as leaders. Many leaders waste a large amount of time, energy, and emotion while being frustrated by the actions of their followers. They react with attempts to command or control their employees. The better response for most leaders is to first adjust their own perspective and approach, and control what they truly can—their own attitude and behaviors. Self-aware leaders increase their effectiveness by continually soliciting feedback, monitoring their behavior, learning about themselves through personality, style, and leadership assessment tools, and evolving their leadership approach.

Insecurity. The harmful behavior of many leaders is often rooted in their own feelings of insecurity and self-doubt which get transferred to others. Few things are more dangerous than an insecure leader! Author Chip Ingram declares "All men are desperately insecure."

Self-awareness is the starting point for leaders to address and overcome the pitfalls of insecurity. Help your leaders to understand and accept their limits so they can move ahead to develop themselves, gain maturity, and lead the development and success of others in positive, collaborative, and encouraging ways.

Others focus. How much of your focus is on yourself versus others? Great leaders find ways to overcome their own selfishness and enhance the lives of others. A great question to test leaders on this is "How is everyone around you doing?" Many leaders would say *"they are doing fine"* when it's obvious that those around them are hurting or failing. You cannot lead without followers, and so your commitment to them is critical. If you can develop a strong sense of how everyone around and connected to you is doing, you will boost your leadership effectiveness.

One simple "others approach" is to consider your stakeholders. Identify all the "people groups" or stakeholders you impact and identify their needs, wants, and expectations. Some of your stakeholder groups might include the following:

- Employees
- Investors
- Customers
- Suppliers
- Resellers
- Distributors
- Volunteers
- Contributors
- Community

Great leaders have a keen awareness of their stakeholders and a strong commitment to satisfy them.

Communication. Great leaders are effective communicators. They not only express their thoughts and plans but also their intentions and emotions. They communicate with heart. Author Darlene Price, in her book *Well Said*, guides leaders by prompting them to communicate *confidently, clearly, concisely, and convincingly*. Heartfelt leadership is expressed person to person, through communication with words, tone, body language, and more. Consider these objectives and questions to communicate wisely:

Clarity and focus—What's most important to communicate at this point in time?
Simple and organized—What method, style, and language will optimize your being understood?

Consistency—How might focus and repetition enhance understanding and absorption?

Integrity and trust—How transparent and genuine are you in your interactions with others?

Expand your leadership potential. Think about the impact of a team with "leaders at all levels" that performs using the *best* of their minds as well as their hearts? What could they accomplish and what obstacles might they overcome? Would you rather compete against or be a part of a team led with great minds *and* hearts? Expand your leadership perspective—and potential—by leading with your heart as well as your mind.

"

One of the most important roles for a leader is to develop great strategy.

"

RBM - Leadership, Strategy, Process advocate

Strategically Planning to Prosper

Do you have a plan? Does your organization, work group, or next project have a written plan to succeed? If so, when was it created? Has it been reviewed and updated within the last three months? Are you using the plan to "focus and allocate" your resources as you originally intended? What are the three most strategic projects you have pending or underway, and how well have you planned for them?

Even a Simple Plan Can Boost the Success of Your Organization, Work Group, or Next Project.

Planning is critical for organizations and project leaders. The degree to which you succeed or fail will likely depend on the effectiveness of your plan. But all too often, we don't invest enough in an up-front strategy that defines the key purposes, parameters, and outcomes that will define our success. Here's some guidance: Allocate at least ten percent of your project resources to develop a strategic plan *before* you take a first step on the journey. Does this sound ridiculous to you, or obvious? If you are not investing adequate resources in planning, you will likely misallocate or waste significant amounts of time, money, and effort. Planning—considering your opportunities as well as your risks—is essential.

Allocate at Least 10% of Your Project Resources to Develop a Strong Strategic Plan Up-Front.

The first challenge for many is how to organize and structure a good plan. An effective plan doesn't need to be complex. Simple is often better. Consider starting with a basic outline and the 80/20 rule. What are the fundamental plan components and the key information (20%) that will provide adequate clarity (80%) without being cumbersome? Use simplicity to your advantage by summarizing your plan on no more than one sheet of paper, using both sides. The result will be a plan with both brevity and substance that helps you communicate the essentials and ensure your success.

Here is a simple step-by-step guide to help you plan strategically:

How to Create a One-Sheet Strategic Plan:

1. Start by summarizing what your organization, work group, or project is about in one carefully written paragraph called your *"About Us."* Use this as your elevator speech, homepage description, recruiting opener, and in other places where you need a brief overview *description*. See if you can keep it to 100 words or less.

2. Identify your *stakeholder groups* and their unique needs, wants, and expectations. Typical groups would be customers, employees, owners, volunteers, suppliers, and your community. What better way to start a plan than with all the people you impact, from their perspective.

3. Clarify the *purpose* of your organization or project, ideally in ten words or less. A clear purpose will describe why you or your project exists and why your stakeholders should care.
4. Paint a picture with words of what a great success would look like and call it your *vision*. Few things are more motivating to those close to you than where you are headed and what's in it for them. Summarize your vision in one short sentence for maximum impact.
5. Identify what value you will provide to your customers and consider it your *mission*. By accomplishing your mission, you can achieve your vision. See if you can summarize your mission to fifteen or fewer words.
6. Create a short list of critical behaviors or considerations, and identify them as your *values* or *beliefs*. Clearly defined values provide guidelines within which successful organizations operate with freedom and empowerment. As tough decisions arise, your values and beliefs will direct you.
7. To achieve your vision, what are some *critical outcomes* or key objectives that you should achieve? A list of five to fifteen of these will provide additional clarity to you and your employees.
8. What are the five to fifteen *indicators* that you can monitor to measure progress toward your objectives? Quantifiable indicators allow "fact-based" decision-making as opposed to emotional decisions triggered by hunches. Determine the best frequency to report on your indicators, such as weekly or monthly.
9. What *goals* can you set for each indicator that would show low/mid/high levels of performance? Goals clarify expectations and show progress toward desired results.

10. Who or what can you observe, study, or otherwise **bench-mark** to learn from and help you visualize what your success may look like? You can avoid many challenges and the risks of pioneering alone by humbly accepting that others have come before who you can learn from.

11. As you identify specific tasks to complete or steps you will need to take, list and sort them into a *prioritized actions* list to help focus and manage your time and resources. Visually monitor your list using simple green/yellow/red highlighting to track your progress and archive all you have accomplished.

Compile and Communicate Your Plan.

Document your plan in a concise format that is easy to create, edit, and share. For a handy, pre-organized one-sheet business plan outline, download the free Plan to Prosper" worksheet at: www. lsp123.com/p2p.

A little planning invested up-front to create a simple strategic outline for your business or next project will reward you nicely with organization, clarity, focus, and a much higher level of success.

"

*A good process step adds
value to the customer.
Otherwise, it's just waste.*

"

Lean Thinking - paraphrased from the book

Better Processes Equal Multiplied Results

Learn to understand, lead, and manage your processes. Every day we experience dozens if not hundreds of processes. When we use a calculator, drive a vehicle, search a topic online, visit an ATM, submit a form, operate a machine, or simply brush our teeth, we perform a process. Some describe a process as a step-by-step procedure. In an organization setting, a more relevant description might be *"a routine that adds value."*

Some processes provide more value than others. If a process is performed well—like when a chef prepares a great meal at a fine restaurant—the result can be amazing. Have you enjoyed the benefit of a high-value process lately? Alternatively, when processes don't work well, their value is diminished or lost completely. Just think of the last automated phone system or waiting line you suffered through! Processes multiply our experiences *for good or for bad.*

Mealtime Example

The processes around us are so numerous and routine, it's easy to overlook their detail and sequence. Just consider the steps to "prepare a meal at home":

1. Purchase ingredients at a store.
2. Transport ingredients home.
3. Stock purchased ingredients.
4. Retrieve select ingredients from storage.
5. Gather cooking tools and utensils.
6. Measure recipe ingredients.
7. Assemble or combine ingredients.
8. Cook or prepare recipe items.
9. Place food on plate and table.
10. Consume the meal.
11. Clean up, wash, and dispose of waste.
12. Store cleaned and unused items.

With all these steps to prepare just one meal, it's no surprise why some restaurants are booming! Customers reward processes that save them time, effort, inconvenience, or otherwise provide value.

Visible and Invisible Processes

Sometimes processes are very visible like in televised sports. In football, for example, we watch the process begin when the ball gets snapped, activating each player to proceed through the sequence of a play. Television sports give us a unique view of process, letting us watch and rewatch the steps or performance—sometimes repeatedly, in slow motion, with the benefit of analysis by expert commentators.

At other times processes happen almost invisibly, like when we "Google" a topic and thousands of references seem to magically appear on our computers within milliseconds. Regardless if visible or behind-the-scenes, customers, spectators, employees, and others will judge our products, services, and organizations by the processes they experience.

Your Role as a Process Leader

One of your most important responsibilities as a leader is to improve processes. Here are four simple steps to help you analyze, develop, manage, and lead processes better:

- Identify
- Implement
- Inspect
- Improve

Identify Your Processes.

To make your processes better, first *identify* them. What are the processes in your workspace, department, or business? Which provide the most value to your customers, clients, employees, and other stakeholders? A good way to identify your processes is to list and organize them into logical groupings. Consider grouping them by sequence, degree of importance, or by value-added contribution. Identify which processes are most critical or essential and list them in priority order.

Identify who owns each process: an individual, a group, or an entire team. Who knows the process or desired outcome the most and is in the best position to develop or make the process better? Does each of your processes have a leader to take responsibility for owning and improving the value they create and results they produce? How well suited are your process owners for the responsibilities that come with that role, including process refinement and evolution? Because the number of processes in most organizations is so large, it is essential to divide ownership and responsibility among your team to ensure that each process is appropriately identified, managed, and supported.

Rob Marchalonis

How Is Each Process Implemented?

Describe and document how you *implement* each process, starting with the most critical. Keep it simple, and begin by using a list, outline, or flow chart. Consider the five Ws (*what, why, who, where, when*) and *how*. *What* is the name of the process? Select a name that will clearly and uniquely describe the process to others. *Why* does the process exist? Is it in sync with the purpose, vision, mission, and values of the organization? *Who*, or what stakeholder groups, are involved in the process: creators, leaders, deliverers, supporters, participants, or recipients? How many stakeholders are involved from each group? *Where* does the process happen? What facilities, equipment, or location-specific needs are required? *When* does the process occur, and are there scheduling, communication, or preparatory steps necessary? Finally, *how* does the process itself happen? What are the sequence steps?

Inspect Your Processes.

Inspect your processes by observing three key process outcomes:

- **Effectiveness**
- **Efficiency**
- **Sustainability**

Is the process *effective*, meaning does it accomplish the desired result? Is the process *efficient*, producing desired results with the best use of resources—time, money, labor, materials, effort, etc.? Is the process *sustainable*, being used, repeated, and duplicated as designed. Frequently, results suffer *not* for lack of a process but rather because the established process is not being followed or sustained.

The Malcolm Baldrige
Performance Excellence Program

Over a period of eleven years, starting in the early 1990s, I studied and learned about organizational excellence through the Malcolm Baldrige Performance Excellence Program. The program was created during the Reagan Presidency and sponsored by NIST in the Commerce Department. For more than a decade my teammates and I at Stoner Inc. participated actively in the program, studying, learning, and engaging via conferences, consultants, benchmarking, award applications, feedback reports, and site visits. Ultimately, we received the Malcolm Baldrige Award in 2003. Only 110 awards have been granted since the program's inception in 1988, and among them only twenty-four were small businesses like ours. Stoner Inc. is the only small business from Pennsylvania to ever receive the award. As an award recipient, we were hosted by the president of the United States George W. Bush in Washington, DC. What an experience! It remains among the top highlights of my career.

The Baldrige Program taught me many lessons, one of which was the importance of process improvement. A classic question from Baldrige experts and examiners is "What's your process to improve your processes?" Honestly, it took me a while to figure out what really was meant by this question. The following was one approach I used to provide an answer, and improve our processes.

Improving Processes

Improve your processes with ongoing *assessment*, *improvement* ideas, and *implementation*. Regularly monitor and measure your processes to *assess* their results. Based on your assessments, what *improvement* ideas can be identified and prioritized to make the process better? Who will *implement* the improvement ideas, how, and by when? Continuous improvement is essential for every process.

- **Assess**
- **Improve**
- **Implement**

Be wary of the "100:10:1 Challenge" with your process stakeholders, which can look something like this: "for every one hundred process assessors *or critics*, often only ten are able—or trained—to provide a legitimate improvement idea, and for each of those only one is empowered—or capable—of implementing the improvement!" *No* process gets better unless it gets assessed, improvement ideas are developed, and those ideas are acted on or implemented. Leaders, your challenge—and opportunity—is to beat the 100:10:1 challenge and achieve better process improvement ratios in your organization.

Multiply Your Results.

On the front lines and in the back rooms of your organization are dozens or even hundreds of processes that are defining your customer's experience. How are you leading and managing them? Use the four Is to Identify, Implement, Inspect, and Improve your processes because better processes equals multiplied results!

LSP123 Resources

As you support your IncentShare workplace, let Leadership, Strategy, and Process (LSP) be your guide. Remember how your leadership and the leadership of those around you can have the most impact on your results. Challenge your leaders to develop great strategy and plans that uniquely position you to satisfy customers much better than your competition. Be mindful of your processes to ensure that they are truly routines that add value.

Altogether, a simple focus on LSP can make your role much easier and satisfying, help you capture opportunities and reach your potential, and share your success with others along the way.

Learn More About LSP and Find Additional Resources At:

www.LSP123.com

Take the Next Step

Has this information been helpful? Are you ready to put an IncentShare plan in place with one or more of your work groups? Developing a plan to share the success of your organization could be the best way to boost the focus, morale, teamwork, and performance of your workforce. Do you have what you need to take the next step?

Need Help? Visit www.IncentShare.com

Go to IncentShare.com for resources and help if and when you might need them.

Send Us Some Feedback.

Please contact us via email at Info@IncentShare.com to share your experience, questions, or concerns as you move forward with IncentSharing.

Best Wishes and Thank You!

*For I know the plans I have
for you, declares the Lord,
plans for welfare and
not for evil, to give you
a future and a hope.*

Jeremiah 29:11 ESV

Notes

1. "Starbucks Fiscal 2015 Form 10-K" (Seattle, WA: Starbucks Corporation, November 12, 2016).

2. Starbucks Coffee Company, "Bean Stock," last modified November 15, 2016, http://starbucksbeanstock.com/en-us/welcome-en-us/about-bean-stock.

3. Strom, Stephanie. "At Chobani, Now It's Not Just the Yogurt That's Rich." The New York Times. April 26, 2016. Accessed March 31, 2017. https://www.nytimes.com/2016/04/27/business/a-windfall-for-chobani-employees-stakes-in-the-company.html?_r=1.

4. J. McGregor, "Apple Opens Up Stock Awards to All Employees—Even Hourly Retail Workers, October 15, 2015, last modified January 13, 2017, https://www.washingtonpost.com/news/on-leadership/wp/2015/10/15/apple-opens-up-stock-awards-to-all-employees-even-hourly-retail-workers/?utm_term=.357c0d7a5b46.

5. McGrath, Maggie. "How The Wells Fargo Phony Account Scandal Sunk John Stumpf." Forbes. October 13, 2016. Accessed March 31, 2017. https://www.forbes.com/sites/maggiemcgrath/2016/09/23/the-9-most-important-things-you-need-to-know-about-the-well-fargo-fiasco/#39dfbd113bdc.

6. A. Mann and J. Harter, "The Worldwide Employee Engagement Crisis," January 7, 2016, accessed September 19, 2016, http://www.gallup.com/businessjournal/188033/worldwide-employee-engagement.

7. A. Adkins, "Majority of U.S. Employees Not Engaged Despite Gains in 2014," January 28, 2015, accessed September 19, 2016, http://www.gallup.com/poll/181289/majority-employees-not-engaged-despite-gains-2014.aspx.

8. J. Rigoni and B. Nelson, "Few Millennials Are Engaged at Work," August 30, 2016, accessed September 19, 2016, http://www.gallup.com/businessjournal/195209/few-millennials-engaged-work.aspx.

9. Employment Situation Summary Table A. Household data, seasonally adjusted, n.d., accessed November 8, 2016, http://www.bls.gov/news.release/empsit.a.htm.

10. Table B-2. Average weekly hours and overtime of all employees on private nonfarm payrolls by industry sector, seasonally adjusted, n.d., last modified November 8, 2016, http://www.bls.gov/news.release/empsit.t18.htm.

11. U.S. Bureau of Labor Statistics, n.d., last modified November 8, 2016, http://www.bls.gov/news.release/pdf/wkyeng.pdf.

12. Barry Schwartz, *Why We Work* (New York: TED Books, Simon & Schuster, 2015).

13. United States Census Bureau, "Nearly 6 Out of 10 Children Participate in Extracurricular Activities," December 9, 2014, accessed January 13, 2017, http://www.census.gov/newsroom/press-releases/2014/cb14-224.html.

14. L. Belling, Writers Dreamtools—Decades—2000, n.d., last modified October 20, 2016, http://www.writersdreamtools.com/view/decades.

15. About Us | Glassdoor, n.d., last modified October 20, 2016, https://www.glassdoor.com/about/index_input.htm.

16. Bureau of Labor Statistics, U.S. Department of Labor, Occupational Outlook Handbook, 2016–17 Edition, Welders, Cutters, Solderers, and Brazers, on the Internet, last modified October 19, 2016, http://www.bls.gov/ooh/production.

17. Salary: Welder | Glassdoor, n.d., last modified October 20, 2016, https://www.glassdoor.com/Salaries/welder.

18. "Walmart 2016 Annual Report." March 30, 2016. Accessed March 31, 2017. http://s2.q4cdn.com/056532643/files/doc_financials/2016/annual/2016-Annual-Report-PDF.pdf.

19. Walmart Salaries | Glassdoor, n.d., last modified October 20, 2016, https://www.glassdoor.com/Salary/Walmart-Salaries-E715.htm.

20. IAAF: World Records, n.d., accessed January 13, 2017, https://www.iaaf.org/records/by-category/world-records.

21. Stoner Baldrige Application, 2003, accessed January 6, 2017, http://patapsco.nist.gov/Award_Recipients/PDF_Files/Stoner_Application_Summary.pdf.

22. Nasdaq October 2016 Volumes, 2016, accessed November 11, 2016, http://ir.nasdaq.com/releasedetail.cfm?ReleaseID=997625.

23. The New York Stock Exchange, n.d., accessed November 11, 2016, https://www.nyse.com/network.

24. Gpickel@pennlive.com, G. P. "How Does James Franklin's Penn State Salary Compare to Other Big Ten, National Coaches?, 2016, accessed January 2, 2017, http://www.pennlive.com/pennstatefootball/index.ssf/2016/10/where_does_james_franklins_pen.html.

25. USA TODAY Sports, n.d., accessed January 2, 2017, http://sports.

26. Djones@pennlive.com, D. J., Penn State football simply can't get by on $36M profit? Blue-White, last bit of PSU charity, issues $20 parking, last modified January 2, 2017, http://www.pennlive.com/pennstatefootball/index.ssf/2016/07/penn_state_athletics_simply_ca.html.

27. USA TODAY Sports, n.d., last modified January 2, 2017, http://sports.

28. Official Athletic Site of Penn State, n.d., last modified January 2, 2017, http://www.gopsusports.com/ot/financial-reports.html.

29. Penn State Athletics Continues to Take Steps to Remain Self-Supporting, n.d., last modified January 2, 2017, http://www.gopsusports.com/genrel/021816aaf.html.

30. PA.Gov, n.d., last modified February 5, 2017, http://
www.penndot.gov/RegionalOffices/district-8/
ConstructionsProjectsAndRoadwork/Pages/Route-11-15-Rock-
Slope-Safety-Improvement.aspx.

31. L. Bock, *Work Rules!: Insights from Inside Google That Will
Transform How You Live and Lead* (New York: Hachette Book
Group, 2015).

32. ECFR—Code of Federal Regulations, n.d., last modified
February 21, 2017, http://www.ecfr.gov/cgi-bin/text-idx?SID=3
e85d53f8182c81fbc6a53d4ce896af2&mc=true&node=pt29.3.7
78&rgn=div5.

33. See note 18 above.

34. Walmart Corporate, n.d., 10 Rules for Building a Business,
last modified October 22, 2016, http://corporate.walmart.com/
our-story/history/10-rules-for-building-a-business.

35. Vilfredo Pareto, n.d., last modified November 11, 2016, https://
en.wikipedia.org/wiki/Vilfredo_Pareto.

Index

Acknowledgments

A long list of wise, talented, and generous people have contributed to the background, content, and compilation of this book. Many others have shared, influenced, and contributed over decades to lessons I've learned and experiences I've enjoyed. My *sincere thanks* go out to:

Shawn Smucker, Rachel Heisey, Mark Griffin, Todd Musso, Blaze Cambruzzi, Rob Skacel, Steve Erb, and my wife, Melissa, who worked diligently with me to edit, enhance, design, and compile multiple drafts of this book.

Family who I love, especially my wife Melissa for her character, smarts, wit, laughter, intuition, patience, and seemingly unwavering support and love; my sons Matthew and Michael who I couldn't be more proud of, keep me younger, are now teaching *me* about leadership, and I miss deeply while they are away; my parents MaryEllen and Bernie, who have taught me (and many others as teachers) priceless life lessons, diligently and generously preserve our family traditions and values, and consistently share their love; my sister Cathy and in-laws Jim, Judy, Ralph, Celeste, Jeff, Leslie, and Madison for fun family times, interesting travel, great meals, and occasional deep discussions.

LSP123 clients and friends for inviting me into your workplace and sharing your challenges and victories with me. Few things give me a bigger thrill than watching *you* grow and succeed.

Former team at Stoner Inc. for an amazing run and all that we were able to do and enjoy together. I learned so much from all of you and appreciate your patience, understanding, and support of me as I learned to be a leader in your midst. I think of you often and fondly.

Extended family and friends, for our relationship and the opportunity to connect, relax, vacation, and share fun times together. Adventures on sand, snow, air, land, sea, and in boats, planes, trains, and cars come to mind.

Church, nonprofit, and volunteer friends for showing me what it means to be a life changed by Christ and the power and joy of unselfish service for the benefit of *others*. You have taught me heartfelt leadership and the importance of relationships along with results.

Vistage, Malcolm Baldrige, KAPE, Lancaster Chamber, and other business community members who taught me many lessons about leadership, strategy, process, and the mutual benefits of volunteering in these circles.

My apologies in advance to anyone I failed to mention here, but know that if you have touched my life, you have had an impact and with very few exceptions, I consider you a blessing.

Thank You!

At least 10% of the profits from this book will be shared with others, specifically with organizations dedicated to improving children's health, welfare, and promoting family strength, self-reliance, and hope through entrepreneurship and microfinance in underserved communities.

Let's All Succeed By Sharing.

About the Author

Rob Marchalonis is the creator of IncentShare and founder of LSP123. More than twenty-five years of experience as CEO, marketing director, engineer, entrepreneur, coach, and consultant has given Rob deep insight into organizational dynamics, motivation, incentives, and sharing to get results. He has advised thousands of leaders in business and nonprofit organizations.

Rob attributes many of his results and blessings to sharing strategies that multiplied sales, profits, productivity, and more. His accomplishments as a leader include twenty years as GM and CEO of Stoner Inc., where he developed business strategy, built a team, and put in place innovative incentive plans that resulted in 15X sales growth. Intimately involved in team development and motivation for most of his career, Rob has spent years developing hundreds of ways to incentivize and share results with individuals, work groups, and entire organizations.

As a business consultant and coach, Rob utilizes both classic and innovative business principles. Many were learned while on an eleven-year journey to achieve the Malcolm Baldrige National Performance Excellence Award from the President of the United States. Others were developed over ten years implementing LEAN enterprise solutions. All were proven while becoming a worldwide supplier and advisor to both small and Fortune 100 customers. While he was CEO of Stoner Inc., the marketing and manufacturing company was named a Best Place to Work in PA for nine years. When you find the right way to "share your success," *everyone* wins!

Why did I write IncentShare? As I work with clients and business leaders, the immediate focus is often on solving employee problems or creating a specific strategy to change employee morale. Too often, there is limited time to learn and understand the *framework* upon which great organizations engage and motivate their workforce. *IncentShare* is intended to help leaders and their teams learn both basic and advanced success-sharing principles so they can grow and prosper. Read *IncentShare* to gain knowledge, discover strategies, and learn incentive tactics to get better results from—and for—your team.

Need help? Each organization has different resources to plan and implement compensation plans. Some of you lead small entrepreneurial companies where just a few employees "wear multiple hats." Others of you have well-staffed human-resource departments with years of training and experience. Regardless, IncentShare can help you no matter if you are well or lightly equipped with staff, experience, and time.

Do you prefer DIY or DIFM? With regard to compensation planning, some of you may prefer to do it yourself (DIY) while others will value a do-it-for-me (DIFM) approach. Whatever your situation or needs, know that we have knowledge, training, and advisors that can make your job easier! We can even look over your current compensation plans to provide feedback and suggest improvement ideas. Consider these IncentShare resources to help you assess, plan, implement, or improve variable compensation plans at your organization:

Here's How IncentShare Can Help You

- Online Resources at IncentShare.com
- Have Your Current Plan Assessed
- IncentShare Starter Kit
- IncentShare Do-It-Yourself Kit
- IncentShare Off-Site Training
- IncentShare On-Site Training
- Expert Phone Consultation
- By-Your-Side Assistance at Your Location
- IncentShare Partnership

The IncentShare approach is primarily focused on variable compensation plans that can be developed for one, several, or all employees in an organization. Variable compensation is typically paid monthly or quarterly through payroll with the amount linked to the performance or results of either a work group or the entire organization.

"

*A journey
of a thousand miles begins
with a single step.*

"

Lao-tzu - Chinese philosopher

Thank You and Best Wishes!

Send us your feedback, questions, or concerns.
Need help? We are eager to hear from you.

Contact us by email at Info@IncentShare.com

IncentShare.com

Succeed by Sharing

IncentShare®

Custom Compensation Plans